Sondheim and *Sweeney Todd*

' … we have some shepherd's pie peppered with actual shepherd on top.'

— Mrs Lovett

Sweeney Todd, the gruesome tale of a murderous barber and his pastry chef accomplice, is unquestionably strange subject matter for the musical theatre — but eight Tony awards and enormous successes on Broadway and the West End testify to its enduring popularity with audiences. Written by Hugh Wheeler, with music and lyrics by Stephen Sondheim, the musical premiered in 1979 and has seen numerous revivals, including Tim Burton's 2007 film version.

Aaron C. Thomas addresses this darkly funny piece with fitting humour, taking on *Sweeney Todd*'s chequered history and genre, its treatment of violence and cannibalism, and its sexual politics.

Aaron C. Thomas is Assistant Professor of Theatre History and Literature at the School of Performing Arts, University of Central Florida, USA.

The Fourth Wall

The Fourth Wall series is a growing collection of short books on famous plays. Its compact format perfectly suits the kind of fresh, engaging criticism that brings a play to life.

Each book in this series selects one play or musical as its subject and approaches it from an original angle, seeking to shed light on an old favourite or break new ground on a modern classic. These lively, digestible books are a must for anyone looking for new ideas on the major works of modern theatre.

www.routledge.com/performance/series/4THW

Also available in this series:

Coming soon:

Sondheim and Wheeler's *Sweeney Todd*

Aaron C. Thomas

Routledge
Taylor & Francis Group

LONDON AND NEW YORK

First published 2018
by Routledge
2 Park Square, Milton Park, Abingdon, Oxon, OX14 4RN

and by Routledge
711 Third Avenue, New York, NY 10017

Routledge is an imprint of the Taylor & Francis Group, an informa business

© 2018 Aaron C. Thomas

The right of Aaron C. Thomas to be identified as author of this work
has been asserted by him in accordance with sections 77 and 78 of the
Copyright, Designs and Patents Act 1988.

British Library Cataloguing-in-Publication Data
A catalogue record for this book is available from the British Library

Library of Congress Cataloging-in-Publication Data
A catalog record for this book has been requested

ISBN: 978-1-138-67886-6 (pbk)
ISBN: 978-1-315-55862-2 (ebk)

Typeset in Bembo
by Out of House Publishing

Contents

Acknowledgements

This is for the friends I've seen and loved in *Sweeney* – Justin Abarca, Elizabeth Triplett, Wahima N. Lino, Ashley Lampson Opstad, Rick Tabor, Caroline Collins, Joseph Ngo, Michael Steger, Michael Fatica and Viveka Bruce. Thanks also to my theatre-going BFF Julie Haverkate, who went with me to see Carolee Carmello and Norm Lewis in *Sweeney* last year. And to my support team while writing this book – Patrick McKelvey, Alexandra Ripp and Ryan M. Davis. Daniel Sack, George Rodosthenous and Ben Piggott all encouraged me to write this volume and have been supportive throughout. Alexandrew Recore and Earl Weaver each read and commented on early chapters. And a special thank you to my friends Jaime Dyson and Meghan Digneit and my students Noah Samotin, Tommy Heller, Jenny Totcky, Kyle Laing and Savannah Rucks, who kindly reviewed the entire manuscript.

Note

All in-text references to *Sweeney Todd* refer to the original 1979 Dodd, Mead & Company edition.

The throat that gleams

The murderous barber Sweeney Todd and his pastry-chef accomplice Mrs Lovett made their first appearances in fiction long before *Sweeney Todd: the Demon Barber of Fleet Street* first appeared on Broadway in 1979. They were not devised by Stephen Sondheim and Hugh Wheeler, neither did they originate as melodramatic caricatures on the British stage. Instead, Sweeney Todd of Fleet Street and Mrs Lovett of Bell Yard first appeared in the columned pages of a type of periodical referred to as a 'penny blood' (the 'penny dreadful' was a later, supposedly more respectable, version of this genre). These short, cheap, easy-to-read publications were aimed at a wide audience of poor and working-class people, and they contained serialized tales, often with criminal subject matter and a vaguely historical setting. The story in which Sweeney first appeared went by the title *The String of Pearls*, and it was published between November of 1846 and March of 1847.[1]

The bloods were penned by various hack writers, working not for artistic fulfilment or literary reputation but for wages earned. Despite its negative connotation, *hack writer* doesn't necessarily have to mean *bad writer*, but these authors often cared little for credit and less for style. Robert Mack, who has written a thorough and fascinating history of the legend of Sweeney Todd, offers two serious candidates for the original author of *The String of Pearls*. These are Thomas Peckett Prest, a novelist and playwright who wrote the stage melodramas *The Miser of Shoreditch* (1854) and *Lucy Wentworth* (1857), and James Malcolm Rymer, an author of penny bloods who typically wrote under various pseudonyms.

Authorship of *The String of Pearls* is disputed and possibly even irrecoverable. As Mack argues, however, even if someone could state definitively whether it was Prest or Rymer (or one of many other candidates) who actually first wrote down the story, legends of barbers who killed unsuspecting patrons, tales of cannibalistic, incestuous families, rumours of pastry shops with suspicious contents and stories of mysterious smells in the crowded urban centres of the eighteenth and nineteenth centuries circulated widely in France, Ireland, England and Italy.[2] The author of *The String of Pearls* – whoever he may have been – cleverly connected the threads of numerous legends together in what quickly became an enduring theatrical narrative, one that would delight and terrify audiences for the next 150 years and beyond.

The String of Pearls found its way from the page to the stage almost immediately:

> Even before the final number [...] had appeared in print on 20 March 1847, a dramatized version of the tale, adapted for the stage by George Dibdin Pitt, was being performed at the Britannia Theatre in High Street, Hoxton, from 22 February of that year – performed, in other words, more than three weeks before the 'original'

narrative in *The People's Periodical* had even had the opportunity to bring the story to its own conclusion.[3]

Like the narrative version of the tale, Dibdin Pitt's *String of Pearls* first appeared in a venue not widely respected for its quality. Food and drink were served inside the Britannia, and audiences could be very rowdy. *Sweeney Todd* has never been quite respectable, and, as we will see, critics were still turning their noses up 132 years later in 1979, when Sondheim and Wheeler's version of the tale premiered at the Uris Theatre in New York, the biggest theatre on Broadway.

Other stage versions of *The String of Pearls* quickly followed Dibdin Pitt's.[4] Although the jewelry in the original title emphasizes the story's love plot, Todd himself was always the real star of the show, and for Frederick Hazleton's 1862 version the play's title became *Sweeney Todd, the Barber of Fleet Street: or, The String of Pearls*. These two stage versions of *Sweeney* cemented some of the standard elements of the show. One could always expect, for example, to see Sweeney Todd and Mrs Lovett, as well as Sweeney's terrified assistant Tobias Ragg (traditionally played by an actress), the young sailor Mark Ingestrie (later renamed Anthony Hope) and his lover Johanna Oakley (she is not traditionally Todd's daughter). In these melodramas Sweeney doesn't generally slit his victims' throats; he uses a trick barber's chair to kill them. A lever opens a trap door, dropping the unsuspecting customer to his death in the cellar. Later – sometimes after waiting as long as a week! – the villain goes downstairs to 'polish off' his victim. Sweeney is an unrepentant villain in these plays, forever threatening to cut someone's throat from ear to ear or gleefully telling the audience that he is excited to polish off some customer or other. *Polish him off* would become one of

Sweeney's typical catchphrases, and almost every subsequent version of the play includes it, though Sondheim and Wheeler leave it out.

Dibdin Pitt and Hazleton established other traditions as well, many of which managed to survive the century between the 1847 original and the 1979 musical. Johanna, for example, always dresses in (male) sailor drag at some point in the show, and Mrs Lovett – as her name implies – is always portrayed as a lustful widow, grotesquely attempting to seduce any number of customers or suitors. The story always takes place in Fleet Street near St Dunstan's Church, and Johanna is nearly always pursued by a hypocritical and libidinous man of the cloth (Hazleton names this character Lupin, 'wolf'). Indeed, even the earliest versions of the play emphasize the hypocrisy of Londoners – men who pretend to be upright but whose righteous pretentions are designed only to mask avarice and lechery.[5] When Sondheim's lyrics seem, perhaps strangely, to celebrate Sweeney sinking his razor into 'the rosy skin / Of righteousness!' (23), punishing 'those / Who moralize!' (2), or 'float[ing] across the throats / Of hypocrites' (67), he directly references this tradition of critical mockery towards the 'moral' and pretentious among us.

The demon barber was always a murderous, unhinged maniac with a disturbingly creepy laugh. By the 1870s his play was being subtitled *The Barber Fiend*,[6] and he is compared to the devil himself in Hazleton's version.[7] The original Sweeney was not a righteous revenger; he was not unjustly imprisoned by a rapacious judge; and he was certainly never a family man. Sweeney Todd was traditionally a thief. That is, although he was most famed for his grisly murders, the motive for these murders was always greed: Sweeney would kill his customers and steal their possessions, including the string of pearls in the play's title. This is true for every stage version of Sweeney Todd from 1847 to 1979, including Malcolm Arnold's *Sweeney Todd* ballet (1959), Brian J. Burton's *Sweeney Todd the Barber: a Melodrama* (1962), Austin Rosser's *Sweeney Todd: a Victorian Melodrama* (1969) and Peter Miller and Randall Lewton's *The Sweeney Todd Shock 'n' Roll Show* (1979).[8] It is this villainous, thieving Sweeney whom we hear described in Sondheim's 'Ballad of Sweeney Todd', when the chorus sings that 'his skin was pale and his eye was odd' (1). It is this traditionally ruthless monster they describe when they sing 'Sweeney was smooth, Sweeney was subtle, / Sweeney would blink and rats would scuttle' (3).

Sweeney Todd is a malicious, unrepentant thief in all versions, that is, but one: Christopher Bond's play *Sweeney Todd: the Demon Barber of Fleet Street*. Bond changed Sweeney's essential character, shifting the murderer's motive from theft to revenge. Bond's Sweeney is also – for the first time – actually an excellent barber, able to shave a face and extract a tooth with dexterity. This Sweeney is a *member* of his nineteenth-century society rather than an external threat to that society.

Dramaturgically speaking, the Dibdin Pitt, Hazleton, Burton and Rosser versions introduce us to a murderer already steeped in crime and vice. Their Sweeneys have few honourable qualities. Bond, however, introduces Sweeney in the company of the eager and honest Anthony Hope, a man who calls Todd 'friend', treats him affectionately, and says that '[he]'ll pray for [his] good fortune'.[9] The very first story we hear in this version is that of Sweeney's false imprisonment, his love for his virtuous wife and his almost deadly escape from an Australian prison colony. Bond's sympathetic introduction teaches the audience how *they* ought to see this new, improved Sweeney, asking us to look at him with compassion rather than distaste.

All of this is a stark contrast to earlier versions of the barber's story, in which we might hear Sweeney telling the audience frankly that 'When a boy, the thirst of avarice was awakened in me by the fair gift of a farthing',[10] while stealing his string of pearls, or unabashedly singing lyrics such as 'When a youth I turned to crime, / And now I'm evil all the time. / I'm evil, I'm evil, as evil can be, / I doubt if there's anyone as evil as me'.[11] Sondheim expressly wanted to avoid this sort of broad characterization, saying that after he had decided to adapt Bond's *Sweeney*, he 'bought all the published versions – which were all terrible'.[12] Bond, too, had found these earlier adaptations in need of 'a heart transplant', and for his play he 'crossed Dumas's *The Count of Monte Cristo* with [...] *The Revenger's Tragedy* for a plot', emphasizing England's class structure and giving his audience a body count worthy of a Jacobean tragedy.[13] Even more importantly, Bond's Sweeney oscillates between motivations, actively fighting with his own desires, confused even about what he wants. In Bond's second act, Sweeney laments 'Farewell! Farewell, Johanna. My dear daughter whom I have not seen these many years. Whose childish laughter I still hear when sleep doth cloy my brain. [...] What would she say now to know her father was a murderer? She must never know, never behold my face'.[14] Bond's Sweeney is a man who can reflect on the person he has become and, although ashamed of his actions, also articulate the tragic futility of his desires. It is this multifaceted, self-reflexive Sweeney – the wronged husband, the imprisoned father, the wounded avenger – whom Sondheim chose as the star of his *Sweeney Todd*.

In a well-known story, Sondheim saw Bond's version in London in 1973 and immediately decided it would make great musical theatre.[15] Sondheim attempted to write the libretto for the show himself but found this difficult, so director Hal Prince suggested that Hugh Wheeler adapt Bond's play.[16] Sondheim's idea was 'a musical horror story, one which would not be sung-through but which would be held together by ceaseless underscoring that would keep an audience in suspense and maybe even scare the hell out of them'.[17] But because Sondheim and Wheeler's *Sweeney* is based on Bond's variant of the story and not one of the others, the musical inherited Bond's sympathetic treatment of his anti-hero and his affection for the characters. The musical's principals – Sweeney, Mrs Lovett, Tobias, Johanna, Lucy and Anthony – are complex, carefully realized figures, and even its villains and charlatans – Turpin and Pirelli, certainly, if not Beadle Bamford and Jonas Fogg – have qualities that raise them above the level of caricature.

This is not to say that that some of *Sweeney*'s characters are not stock figures. Johanna and Anthony are the typical heterosexual couple of nineteenth-century melodrama, falling in love at first sight and escaping daringly from the villains. Tobias, too, is a stock figure of melodrama, the hopeful innocent trapped by difficult circumstances – similar to the guileless mute Florio in Pixérécourt's *The Forest of Bondy* (1814), Paul, the trusting enslaved boy in Boucicault's *The Octoroon* (1859), or Jonas, the gullible orphan in Wheeler's own melodrama *We Have Always Lived in the Castle* (1966). And if Sweeney Todd himself is a revenger whom we might compare to Hamlet (as Erika Munk does), then our protagonist, too, is a stock character – the 'malcontent' of Elizabethan and Jacobean tragedy who metes out violent judgment on his society.[18]

Stock characters, however, are simply types, and those types can be more or less complex depending on the skill of those who put them to use. Excellent writers can help us see old theatrical types in new and intriguing ways. Bond's *Sweeney Todd* shifted the Sweeney story, reinterpreting it as a study in madness, revenge, capitalism and class conflict. Sondheim and Wheeler's *Sweeney Todd* also reinterpreted the US American musical, garnering a range of responses from laudatory to condemnatory and prompting the *New York Post*'s Clive Barnes to say that 'If you have any interest in the musical theater you must see *Sweeney Todd*. It is not just next month's cocktail party conversation – it will be talked about for years'.[19] Barnes, as it turns out, was right.

'The throat that gleams', the title of this chapter, is a nod to the eponymous string of pearls under which the legend of Sweeney Todd used to play on the London stage. The remainder of this book will be divided into three further chapters: 'The throat that sings' will describe *Sweeney Todd*'s genre and its relationship to other theatre traditions; 'The throat that bleeds' will address the show's treatment of violence; and 'The throat that swallows' will discuss both *Sweeney*'s erotics and its use of the metaphor of cannibalism.

A thorough discussion of *Sweeney*'s music – its tribute to Bernard Herrmann's score for *Hangover Square*, its manipulation of the *Dies Irae* and its debts to Stravinsky, Berg and others – is beyond the scope of this little book. Fortunately, several musicologists have undertaken this work, and Sondheim himself has discussed *Sweeney*'s music extensively.[20] This book focuses, instead, on the themes in *Sweeney Todd* and on the connections the musical makes with theatre traditions and mythology. I aim, always, to think of a piece of theatre as a living, changeable thing – Sondheim has repeatedly encouraged directors' novel takes on his material – and so I imagine this book, more than anything else, as an extended essay on *Sweeney Todd*'s provocations and ideas, one that might push new productions of the show in unexpected directions.

Notes

1 Robert L. Mack, *The Wonderful and Surprising History of Sweeney Todd: the Life and Times of an Urban Legend* (London: Continuum, 2007), 139–148. See also Robert L. Mack, ed., *Sweeney Todd: the Demon Barber of Fleet Street* (Oxford: Oxford University Press, 2007).

2 Mack, *Wonderful*, 148–194.

3 Mack, *Wonderful*, 107.

4 For a chronology of Sweeney Todd narratives see Daniel Gerould, "A Toddography," *New York Literary Forum* 7: 43–48 or Mack, *Sweeney*, xxxi–xxxvii.

5 See George Dibdin Pitt, *The String of Pearls (Sweeney Todd)*, in *The Golden Age of Melodrama: Twelve 19th Century Melodramas*, edited by Michael Kilgarriff (London: Wolfe, 1974), 237–276 and Frederick Hazleton, *Sweeney Todd, the Barber of Fleet Street: or, The String of Pearls* (London: Samuel French, 1862), 8.

6 Dibdin Pitt 263.

7 Hazleton 4.

8 Peter Miller and Randall Lewton, *The Sweeney Todd Shock 'n' Roll Show* (London: Samuel French, 1980).

9 Christopher G. Bond, *Sweeney Todd: the Demon Barber of Fleet Street* (London: Samuel French, 1974), 1–2.

10 Austin Rosser, *Sweeney Todd: a Victorian Melodrama* (London: Samuel French, 1971), 6.

11 Brian J. Burton, *Sweeney Todd the Barber: a Melodrama* (London: Samuel French, 1962), 27.

12 Robert Berkvist, "Stephen Sondheim Takes a Stab at Grand Guignol," *New York Times*, 25 February 1979, D5.

13   Christopher G. Bond, "Introduction," in *Sweeney Todd: the Demon Barber of Fleet Street* by Stephen Sondheim and Hugh Wheeler (New York: Applause, 1991), 3–4.

14   Bond, Sweeney, 31.

15   Stephen Sondheim, *Finishing the Hat: Collected Lyrics (1954–1981) with Attendant Comments, Principles, Heresies, Grudges, Whines and Anecdotes*, (New York: Knopf, 2010), 311–312.

16   Gretchen Cryer, "On Collaboration between Authors and Directors," *Dramatists Guild Quarterly* 16, no. 2 (1979): 23.

17   Sondheim, *Finishing the Hat*, 312.

18   Erika Munk, "Sondheim, Bloody Sondheim," *Village Voice*, 12 March 1979, 85.

19   Clive Barnes, "Sondheim's *Sweeney Todd* Is a Bloody Good Musical," *New York Post*, 2 March 1979, 29.

20   See Carey Blyton, "Sondheim's *Sweeney Todd*: the Case for the Defence," *Tempo* 149 (1984): 19–26; Alfred Mollin, "Mayhem and Morality in *Sweeney Todd*," *American Music* 9, no. 4 (1991): 405–417; Stephen Banfield, *Sondheim's Broadway Musicals* (Ann Arbor: University of Michigan Press, 1993), 281–310; Steve Swayne, *How Sondheim Found His Sound* (Ann Arbor: University of Michigan Press, 2005); Raymond Knapp, *The American Musical and the Performance of Personal Identity* (Princeton: Princeton University Press, 2006); Mark Eden Horowitz, *Sondheim on Music: Minor Details and Major Decisions*, 2nd edn (Lanham: Scarecrow Press, 2010), 125–153; Stephen Banfield, "Sondheim's Genius," in *The Oxford Handbook of Sondheim Studies*, edited by Robert Gordon (Oxford: Oxford University Press, 2014), 11–24.

2

The throat that sings

Clive Barnes was sure that Sondheim and Wheeler's *Sweeney Todd* would be talked about for years to come, and indeed the show has become a classic. Its original production won eight Tony Awards, and it has been revived repeatedly in New York, London and elsewhere. Hal Prince's original production was recorded for television in 1980 – with Angela Lansbury, the original Mrs Lovett, and George Hearn as Sweeney. Director Tim Burton made *Sweeney* into an Academy Award-winning film in 2007 (with Johnny Depp and Helena Bonham Carter), and the show has been recorded for television an additional two times, once with Hearn and Patti LuPone in 2001 and again with Bryn Terfel and Emma Thompson in 2015, both directed by Lonny Price. There are also audio recordings of the original 1979 production, the 2000–2001 concert production, John Doyle's 2005 Broadway revival (with LuPone and Michael Cerveris) and a 2012 Jonathan Kent production with Michael Ball and Imelda Staunton – and that's in addition to the mostly unlistenable movie soundtrack. (With such a wealth of alternative recordings, I really shouldn't complain, but it is difficult to resist.)

When *Sweeney Todd* first premiered, however – in New York in 1979 and in London in 1980 – reviews were not uniformly warm. Many critics, in fact, were extraordinarily hostile. Take Harold Clurman as an example: the esteemed director wrote in the *Nation* that 'the entire production possesses very little substance. The satiric point is not pungent, the terror not scary, the comedy rather ugly, the texture dense without expressing anything but cleverness'.[1] In the *Village Voice*, Erika Munk said that 'When I saw the play I felt a kind of stunned loathing', adding that 'Even the gore is trimmed – I've had better thrills in a wax museum'.[2] The *New Republic*'s Stanley Kauffmann was also less than thrilled. He noted that 'Everything scary is telegraphed and the throat-cuttings (many of them) so much like an abattoi[r] instead of sheer madness, that bored disgust arises, not horror'.[3]

The harshest of the reviews were much worse. In London's *Sunday Times*, James Fenton called the show 'pretentious and fatuous', complaining that

> Sweeney Todd the musical is, if one can imagine such a thing, a tissue of bullshit from start to finish. Don't be deceived by the talk of Sweeney Todd serving a dark and hungry God. God is dragged in by the heels, kicking and screaming for the sake of a rhyme. […] Mrs Lovett couldn't give a damn about the barber's victims. Nor could Stephen Sondheim and nor could Hal Prince. If they didn't pretend to care one would leave the musical feeling, well, that was a massively tasteless exercise, but never mind. The pretentiousness has been introduced in an attempt to keep down the tastelessness, in rather the same way as people put goats into graveyards in order to keep down the weeds.[4]

Michael Feingold saw the production as an exercise in hostility towards its audience, opining that 'when Mrs. Lovett serves her cannibal pies to a chorus thundering out banally enthusiastic phrases, it is impossible to miss the analogy to an artist and his uncomprehending appreciators'.[5] John Lahr even wrote a six-page jeremiad in *Harper's* claiming that, with *Sweeney*, 'Death is now resolutely Sondheim's dominion; but even his appetite for blood is bloodless'. In Lahr's judgment, 'Sondheim's cold elegance matches the spiritual pall that has settled over American life. His musicals are chronicles in song of the society's growing decrepitude. They foreshadow the newest barbarism – a nation that has no faith in the peace it seeks or the pleasure it finds'.[6] Not that Lahr had seen the show; he hadn't.

To be fair, *Sweeney* also had its defenders among the critics. Clive Barnes, as I noted above, thought the show was 'terrific' and 'a bloody good musical'.[7] In a column published beside Feingold and Munk in the *Voice*, Julius Novick said the American theatre needed more shows with emotions on an operatic scale like *Sweeney*.[8] Writing for the *Daily News*, Rex Reed was truly carried away, labelling *Sweeney* 'one of those rare, extraordinary, and awesome spectacles like the Aurora Borealis or the Valley of the Kings':

> I don't think serious theatregoers have ever seen anything quite like it, and I don't think I, for one, will ever see its equal again. It is epic, monumental, staggering – a work of such scope and vision and daring that it dwarfs every other Broadway musical that attempts even to invite comparison.[9]

Reed also thought the show 'might possibly be years ahead of its time', and, indeed, the vitriol of many of *Sweeney*'s early critics does seem rather baffling from a twenty-first-century vantage point. Even John Lahr later changed his tune. He still objects to the post-Sondheim musical, which he refers to as an 'attenuated' version of the form, but he was entranced by John Doyle's 2005 revival of *Sweeney*, calling it 'luminous and a sort of landmark'.[10]

A large part of the reason why critics originally had such a problem with the show is that it did not easily fit within an established musical theatre genre. John Simon, who thought *Sweeney* 'a historic event on Broadway', nevertheless objected to what he saw as Sondheim and Wheeler's attempt to blend Grand Guignol, melodrama and 'ultrasophisticated musicalization distinctly aspiring to opera'. Simon found the show inconsistent, 'like a mad dinner party at which the dessert interrupts the hors d'oeuvre and the pousse-café is poured into the soup'.[11] In the *New York Times* Walter Kerr wondered 'Is this parodied Victorian melodrama, meant essentially to be laughed at? Or is it, as the program suggests, a "musical thriller," meant to chill?'.[12] For Martyn Sutton, *Sweeney* is an

> amalgam of various theatrical styles: Greek Tragedy, Victorian Melodrama, Grand Guignol and Broadway Musical. […] Furthermore – the operatic-style numbers are reminiscent of Brecht and [Weill], Sweeney Todd clearly bearing a marked resemblance to Mack the Knife. In short: the show is easier to appreciate than it is to define.[13]

As Sondheim said much later, '*Sweeney Todd* has been called by people who care about categories everything from an opera to a song cycle'.[14]

Critics and scholars have continued to debate about the genre to which *Sweeney Todd* belongs. Entire academic articles, in fact, are dedicated to discussion of whether the show is 'really' an opera or not.[15] I will not dwell on this question – readers interested in the debate may refer to Blyton (1984) and Banfield (1993) – but I think it worth noting that the most frequently cited points of comparison suggested for *Sweeney Todd* are Greek tragedy, Jacobean tragedy, the Grand Guignol and the Brecht–Weill collaborations of the late 1920s and early 1930s. Comparisons to these genres can help us to think through the way *Sweeney* works, by which I mean *why Sweeney works so very well*. Indeed, it is striking that these comparisons all refer to genres that were successful in so many various periods of time, ancient, early modern, modern and avant-garde. In this chapter I will briefly discuss some of the qualities of each of these theatrical genres in order to draw out some of the ways that connecting them with *Sweeney Todd* can help us make sense of Sondheim and Wheeler's musical thriller.

Sweeney Todd might seem, on the surface, to compare easily with Greek (or, rather, Athenian) tragedy, a genre which surfaced in the sixth century BCE and thrived until the late fourth century BCE. Athenian tragedies most notably featured a singing, dancing chorus that functioned as an integral part of the narrative itself. *Sweeney Todd*'s ensemble does not function like this ancient Greek chorus. The various 'Ballad of Sweeney Todd' sequences serve, not as part of the plot – as a Greek chorus would – but as a narrative frame, and the members of the musical's chorus are apparently unaffected by the action of *Sweeney Todd* itself.

For some critics, the important link between *Sweeney* and ancient drama is something the Athenians called tragic *necessity*. Joanne Gordon, who compares Sweeney to Sophocles' Philoctetes, says that

> [Sweeney's death] is not the arbitrary death of melodrama but the necessary death of tragedy. The question of Sweeney's moral regeneration remains moot. Unlike traditional melodrama, Sondheim's *Sweeney Todd* lacks the unambiguous idealistic certainty of the simplistic tract. Good and evil, right and wrong, are not clearly defined in the emotional torment of the protagonist.[16]

In other words, unlike in melodrama, a form in which the protagonist is often redeemed and frequently finds himself promising to be a better man at play's end, Sondheim and Wheeler never wonder whether their main character will redeem himself. Instead, Sweeney moves towards vengeance – and towards his own annihilation – according to the law of divine necessity followed by ancient playwrights and described by classicists like William Arrowsmith and Bernard Williams. Sweeney does not merely 'serv[e] a dark and a vengeful god' (3); rather his fate seems to be demanded by that god, by the 'pitiless, daemonic, necessitous power' Euripides stages in plays such as his *Bacchae* and *Heracles*.[17]

Melodrama, as we will see, is filled with complexity and contradiction, so Gordon is incorrect to describe melodrama as 'simplistic' or to ascribe to it an 'unambiguous idealistic certainty', but her argument about Sweeney's tragic necessity is borne out by the text. During 'Epiphany' – at the moment in the play when fate seems completely to have deserted him – Sweeney speaks in the very language of necessity. 'I will have vengeance, / I will have salvation!', he says. He uses the simple future tense *I'll* or *I will* repeatedly here: 'And I'll never see Johanna, / No, I'll never hug my girl to me'; 'I will have you!'; 'And I *will* get him back / Even as he gloats / In the meantime I'll practice / On less honorable throats' (94–95). Sweeney describes what *will happen*, and he is correct. Fate, in other words, has not deserted Sweeney during 'Epiphany'; it rather works *through* him. The work that awaits Sweeney at the end of the song is the work of the infernal machine of Athenian tragedy, the playing out of necessity.

As we saw earlier, Christopher Bond consciously used Jacobean tragedy as a model for his *Sweeney Todd*, adapting themes and plot points from Middleton's *The Revenger's Tragedy*. 'Jacobean' is properly a term denoting a time period rather than a genre – specifically the two decades (1603–1625) in England under the rule of King James I after the death of Queen Elizabeth I. But the designation has come to describe a bloodthirsty and 'decadent' quality associated with the drama of that era and even more particularly that drama's seeming obsession with the theme of revenge. These qualities appear in plays such as Webster's *The Duchess of Malfi*, Tourneur's *The Atheist's Tragedy*, Middleton's *Women Beware Women*, Beaumont and Fletcher's *The Maid's Tragedy*, Chapman's *Bussy D'Ambois* and Marston's *Antonio's Revenge*, tragedies that boast intricate plots, numerous narrative twists and final acts littered with corpses.

The Jacobean dramatists seem obsessed both with spying and with nefarious tactics for revenge. Their plays are filled with plans gone awry and murderers hoisted, as it were, with their own petards. These tragedies are also famous for their fifth-act bloodbaths, and, like his vengeful seventeenth-century brothers and sisters, Sweeney is responsible for the high body count in his story, himself becoming one of the killed at play's end.

I have already noted that the character of Sweeney Todd functions in ways similar to the stock malcontent figure of Jacobean tragedy, but it is also worth drawing out the reasons for the discontent harboured by these characters. The malcontents in these plays do not see the world as an inherently unhappy place; they rather see their societies as having been *made* unfair through the corruption, avarice and false morality of those in power. So Bosola, the malcontent of *The Duchess of Malfi*, can complain that 'places in the court are but like beds in the hospital, where this man's head lies at that man's foot, and so lower and lower',[18] and Vindice, the revenger of *The Revenger's Tragedy*, can assume the disguise of a pimp, calling himself 'a right man then, a man o'th' time; / For to be honest is not to be i'th' world'.[19] It is not difficult to hear an echo of these complaints in Sweeney's statement of dissatisfaction with the society in which he lives: 'There's a hole in the world / Like a great black pit / And the vermin of the world / Inhabit it' (9). The hole Sweeney describes 'goes by the name of London', the same corrupt city the Jacobean dramatists were reproaching in the seventeenth century (9).

Sweeney's grievances, like those of the Jacobean malcontents, are not with existence *per se* but with the corrupt and vicious men who control society, those 'privileged few, / Making mock of the vermin / In the lower zoo, / Turning beauty into filth and greed' (9). Indeed, Bosola's analogy for corrupt power in *The Duchess of Malfi*, in which one man's head lies at another man's feet, is an image Sweeney repeats precisely in 'Epiphany' when he describes the 'two kinds of men' in the world: 'There's the one staying put / In his proper place / And the one with his foot / In the other one's face' (94). Sweeney, like the malcontents of Jacobean tragedy, sees civilization as a place of greed and decay.[20]

Like Jacobean tragedy, the Grand Guignol is also infamous for its high body counts and gruesome images. This theatre of horror was known for its realistic presentations of violence, troubling stories of psychological terror and flair for 'true crime' narratives. Commentators writing about *Sweeney* have been prone to discussing the Grand Guignol as though it were identical to melodrama,[21] but the two forms are from different time periods entirely and are related only by the fact that both were immensely popular in their respective historical moments.

The Théâtre du Grand-Guignol was founded in Paris in 1897 by the Naturalist writer Oscar Méténier. Initially, Méténier's theatre was 'not a theatre of horror *per se*, but a successful house of naturalism, dedicated to the true-to-life representation of a society dehumanized by capitalism and bourgeois morality'.[22] The Théâtre du Grand-Guignol told stories of the French working class while criticizing conventional, middle-class morality. In 1899, however, this theatre was taken over by producer Max Maurey, who established it as a successful theatre of horror. Maurey even claimed to have hired a house doctor who would care for theatre patrons who fainted or became ill because of a play's subject matter. The Grand-Guignol became 'a popular theatre with its distinctive programming, acting and production style, with a loyal team of actors, writers and audiences members'.[23] The term *Grand Guignol* itself became shorthand for any play with realistically staged violence designed to terrify its audiences.

This Parisian theatre of thrills (which spawned a tamer London version hampered by censorship) developed a trademark style known as '*la douche écossaise*, a "hot and cold shower" of dramatic pieces interspersed with comedies'.[24] Short plays with horrific subject matter would alternate with farcical one-act pieces, giving the audience a break from dramatic intensity and convincing them to let their guard down before terrifying them yet again. If it makes sense for us to refer to *Sweeney Todd* as Grand Guignol because of the gruesome spurts of fake blood jetting out of Sweeney's prop razor, we might also do well to note that Sondheim and Wheeler's musical actually follows the *dramaturgical* structure of a Grand Guignol programme. As Raymond Knapp puts it, *Sweeney*

> develops a pattern of first scaring the hell out of its audi-
> ence and then rescuing the situation through humor,
> each time by introducing Mrs. Lovett into a situation
> saturated with Sweeney Todd's wrenching angst. This
> scare–rescue pattern happens twice to great effect, at the
> beginning and end of Act I, but its real payoff is the dev-
> astating conclusion, where there is no comic rescue.[25]

Sondheim and Wheeler deliberately alternate between humour and terror throughout *Sweeney Todd*; Mrs Lovett is not the only comic figure. Consider the absurd nonsense of the Beadle's harmonium sequence – right before he is killed – or the farcical business of Pirelli's disembodied hand trying to alert Tobias of his own murder. These uses of the 'hot and cold shower' have less to do with the catharsis or release (appar-ently) promised by Aristotle's version of Athenian tragedy (*pace* Gordon[26]) and much more to do with the practical scare tactics developed by the artists at the Grand-Guignol.

The juxtaposition of farce and drama in *Sweeney Todd* may also point us towards the work of Bertolt Brecht, who, in his discussion of *The Rise and Fall of the City of Mahagonny* (1930) argued 'that a certain unreality, irrationality and lack of seriousness should be introduced at the right moment, and so strike with a double meaning'.[27] The irrationality Brecht describes here is designed not to scare his audience but to comment ironically on the play's more serious action in order to teach.

Academics and popular critics alike have found similarities between *Sweeney* and the collaborations of Brecht and Kurt Weill, especially *Mahagonny*, *The Threepenny Opera* (1928) and *The Seven Deadly Sins* (1933).[28] We will discuss Brecht more fully in the final chapter on cannibalism, but we can note here, as an *amuse bouche*, that Brecht frequently used metaphors of eating to describe musical theatre as a form. He warns us in his essay 'The Modern Theatre Is the Epic Theatre' that '*Mahagonny* may not taste particularly agreeable; it may even (thanks to a guilty conscience) make a point of not doing so. But it is culinary through and through'.[29] Brecht and Weill's show is designed, in other words, for consumption, even if the audience leaves with a bad taste in its mouth. One hears an echo of the very same worry in Angela Lansbury's discussions of *Sweeney Todd*'s original production. Lansbury, in fact, uses the same gustatory metaphor: '"We loved doing the show," Angela says, "and I did believe in it, but I could see that audiences were having a tough time swallowing it"'.[30] The puns seem simply to write themselves.

It is also worth noting that what many of us understand by the term 'Brechtian' actually describes several, quite different, theatrical techniques, including, but not limited to, self-conscious theatricality, music that comments on a play's action rather than supporting it, writing that emphasizes Marxist social criticism, stripped-down or spare production values, alienation effects (which ask an audience to look at the world in new ways), acting with an ironic or detached performance style, an engaged treatment of the historical context of a story, an undermining of plot or narrative and an emphasis on the ability of human beings to make decisions that alter their circumstances. Not all Brecht–Weill collaborations involved all of these techniques, of course, and if *Sweeney Todd* is 'Brechtian', it, too, uses some of these techniques and avoids others. *Sweeney* is, for example, undoubtedly interested in some variety of social criticism, but it does not use music that ironizes the story, is mostly uninterested in historical context, and does not attempt to inspire detached reflection. On the contrary, *Sweeney* is, above all, a narrative, designed to surprise and thrill its audience.

Of course, since we are describing delights, surprises and thrills, the form that should come immediately to mind is *melodrama*, that favourite whipping boy of genres, that 'guttersnipe of dramatic forms', as Daniel Gerould puts it.[31] Although *melodramatic* is a descriptor often used pejoratively in regard to any performance of excess or emotion, the term properly describes a theatrical form combining music and theatre: *mélo-drame*, as it was originally coined. This musical theatre genre – the most popular form of theatre in the USA, UK and Europe throughout the nineteenth century – had specific characteristics on which an audience could depend when attending a performance. These were, among others, an appeal to the audience's emotions through musical underscoring; an incorporation of song and dance within the plot; the narrative use of coincidences, concealed identities and stunning reversals; an emphasis on plot rather than character or theme; the use of comic relief, often provided by a 'foreign' or racialized figure; the theme of feminine virtue beset by wickedness, frequently involving an attempted sexual violation; and – usually but not always – a happy ending for a romantic couple. Plays such as John Augustus Stone's

Metamora (1829), Louisa Medina's *Ernest Maltravers* (1838), George Aiken's *Uncle Tom's Cabin* (1852) and Augustin Daly's *Under the Gaslight* (1867) exemplify the genre in the USA.

As we saw in the previous chapter, stage versions of *Sweeney Todd* have almost exclusively been constructed as melodramas. They nearly all include musical underscoring, sequences of broad farce, surprising reversals (Mark Ingestrie usually comes back from the dead), besieged virtue (a villain almost always attempts to rape/marry Johanna) and a happy ending for the romantic couple.

Sondheim and Wheeler's version is perfectly in keeping with these melodramatic traditions. *Sweeney* was originally conceived as a play that would be thoroughly underscored by music,[32] and Sondheim himself has extensively written about their show as a melodrama.[33] In addition to the continuous underscoring, *Sweeney* incorporates (with Mrs Lovett's songs) the type of music-hall tunes on which melodrama often relied. *Sweeney* also depends for some of its comic relief on a foreigner with a dubious command of English (Pirelli, in fact, has two *different* accents!), a staple of the melodramatic form. As for plot twists, *Sweeney* is filled with them; the musical's complicated finale incorporates one surprising reversal after another.

If critics were puzzled about the precise genre in which *Sweeney Todd* belonged, then, this confusion was mostly wilful, and we can also attribute it, at least partially, to the snobbery that has *always* accompanied critical disapproval of melodrama. Genre confusion has veritably defined melodrama, so that, if it is up for debate exactly what kind of musical *Sweeney Todd* is, it might in fact be best described precisely by its generic bastardy, its insistence on combining violence and music, romance and comedy. From the first, melodrama was

understood as neither tragedy nor comedy but the illegit-
imate child of the two. But it is critics, not audiences, who
tend to insist on generic purity. Combining seriousness and
laughter with song and dance, melodrama was an extremely
popular but always disrespected form that dared indecently to
exceed genre itself.

Classifying the musical as a melodrama allows us to attend
to an essential aspect of *Sweeney* that is often ignored in
both popular and critical discussion, a feature of the show
that is indispensable to its success as a melodrama: Anthony
and Johanna's romance. Although their happy ending is
overshadowed in the play's epilogue by Sweeney's return from
the dead, the two lovers apparently find happiness with each
other at the story's end. More importantly, their love for each
other and desire to be together is one of the driving forces of
Sweeney's plot.

For Sondheim the emphasis in *Sweeney* was always terror
and suspense; Bond, in contrast, always wanted *Sweeney* to
be funnier. Carol Ilson says that it was Harold Prince who
'moved the show more and more toward the romantic, partly
as a balance for the gory material'.[34] Foster Hirsch quotes
Prince as saying that 'To make that kind of show work, you
have to write romantic music [...]. Our aim was to make the
score as lush as we could'; Hirsch concludes that 'Many of the
show's ballads, like "Green Finch and Linnet Bird," "Johanna,"
"Not While I'm Around," and "Pretty Women" are among
the richest and most soaring Sondheim has yet written'.[35]

Theatrical melodrama requires a romantic couple, and
Sweeney Todd depends on a heroic young man intent on
rescuing an ingénue whose virtue is besieged by lecherous
villains. In Bond's version of *Sweeney*, this portion of the
plot is described by Anthony *after* he has seen Johanna for

the first time, and the audience does not meet the young lady herself until the Judge proposes marriage. In Sondheim and Wheeler's version, in contrast, the audience sees Johanna at her window before Anthony does, and we briefly get to know her as a character prior to the love plot itself. Johanna sings about and to a bunch of caged songbirds, a metaphor for the young woman's desire for freedom that is also unique to Sondheim and Wheeler's version of the tale.

By way of concluding this chapter, I want to spend some time with this first of *Sweeney Todd*'s romantic songs. Not only is 'Green Finch and Linnet Bird' a much more multifaceted song than has been assumed, but also its lyrical complexity is an excellent reminder that melodrama itself can be metaphorically rich just as often as it can be frivolous. Sondheim and Wheeler, in Johanna's opening song, ask us to take their ingénue – and their melodrama – seriously.

The birds Johanna describes in 'Green Finch' are quite plainly intended as a metaphor for her own situation; indeed, Sweeney himself will refer to his daughter as 'my turtledove, my dear' in act two (128). Johanna recognizes her own house as a cage, one that has 'many rooms / Damask and dark', and she asks the captive birds to teach her how to sing despite their mutual incarceration (25). Johanna, as it happens, remains confined for most of *Sweeney Todd*; imprisonment is one of the show's central thematic preoccupations, one which Prince's original production emphasized and which we will discuss more fully in the next chapter. The caged birds in Kearney's Lane, then, are an image of song and flight, of beauty and love, but they also reflect the show's larger themes.

A ringdove, like the turtledove to which Sweeney compares Johanna, is a symbol of monogamy and romantic affection.

Larks, too, are known as a symbol of lovers (as well as a food source). But the other birds on Johanna's list have meaningful associations with the more sinister elements of *Sweeney Todd*. As any young reader of Mother Goose could tell you, blackbirds – four and twenty of them, no less – were once proverbially baked into a (meat) pie. It is worth remarking, too, that 'when the pie was opened / the birds began to sing', which means that the birds were baked *alive* into the pie. Of course, the blackbirds do not die in the oven, living long enough for one of them to nip off (but not eat) the nose of the maid as she is in the garden hanging out the clothes.

Johanna's other birds contain further references to brutal violence or outrageous gastronomy. Linnet birds, robinets and greenfinches are all familially related, part of a group of similarly beaked, seed-eating songbirds. Linnets get their name from their fondness for eating linseed or flax. The robinet, also called the blue chaffinch, is probably most famous for having been memorialized in Thomas Hardy's poem 'The Blinded Bird', which laments the practice of blinding birds. Hardy's poem is similar in both sentiment and content to Johanna's song:

> So zestfully canst thou sing?
> […]
> Blinded ere yet a-wing
> By the red-hot needle thou,
> I stand and wonder how
> So zestfully thou canst sing![36]

The birds in *Sweeney* have also been blinded, and this act of barbarism is uniquely included in Sondheim and Wheeler's version.

Perhaps the most famous finch (or at least it was thought to be a finch until only very recently) is the ortolan, a bird that is a culinary delicacy in France. Robert Mack reports that, in one of 'the earliest references to the story in English that eventually became the core narrative of Sweeney Todd', a baker is making pies, 'the flavour and crust of which were uncommonly gratifying'.[37] The pies in this story turn out to be filled with the flesh of young children, but topping the list of suggestions for the pies' mysterious contents are veal and ortolans, with their peculiar flavour. In France, there is an entire tradition for how to cook, serve and eat ortolans. The birds are trapped and then kept in covered cages so that they gorge themselves on millet. Ancient Romans were even rumoured to have blinded the birds – like Sondheim and Wheeler's bird-seller – so that they ate to excess. Once fattened, ortolans are drowned alive in Armagnac and then roasted whole, with their heads attached. They are also served and consumed whole – bones and all – with the diner traditionally covering his own head with a napkin. The traditional function of the napkin is to hide the hubris of this gastronomic act from the gods and also, apparently, to enhance the richness of the dish.[38] However, it is more likely that this covering of the face indicates an ancient taboo: famed anthropologist Sir James George Frazer describes numerous groups of people who hid their faces while eating or drinking. This was done to prevent spirits from entering the body and to guard against the evil eye.[39]

Birds do not normally feature in versions of *Sweeney* (a loyal hound appears more often), but Sondheim and Wheeler's is not actually the first to incorporate birdsong into its music. Near the end of Malcolm Arnold's 1959 ballet *Sweeney Todd*, the percussionists are instructed that 'a nightingale should be played as loudly as possible'.[40] The musical effect, clearly audible on any recording of Arnold's piece, is strikingly similar to the transition in Sondheim's music between the first reprise of 'The Ballad of Sweeney Todd' and the first bars of 'Green Finch and Linnet Bird'.[41] The nightingale is the bird that resonates most powerfully with the themes of *Sweeney Todd*, for the nightingale is linked with the ancient myth of Procne and Philomela.

In the *Metamorphoses*, Ovid tells the story of Procne, a princess of Athens who marries Tereus of Thrace. After several years of marriage and the birth of a son, Itys, Procne persuades Tereus to sail south to bring her sister Philomela for a visit. Tereus goes to Athens, but on the return voyage he rapes his sister-in-law. Philomela is outraged, vowing to tell the world of his violence. In order to silence her, Tereus cuts out Philomela's tongue and rapes her again. Ovid's descriptions of Philomela's mutilation and of the violence of the rape itself are graphic and powerful. After a period of time, Philomela finds a way to tell her sister that Tereus has raped her, and in a shocking act of revenge, Procne murders their son, butchers his body, and feeds little Itys to Tereus for dinner. Weeping and wretched, Tereus attacks the sisters, but they fly away, transformed into birds, one into a nightingale and the other into a swallow: 'And even now their breasts / Retain the marks of the slaughter, and their feathers / Are stained with blood'.[42]

Johanna's evocation of the nightingale in *Sweeney* is a poetic link, relating the melodrama's romantic plot first to the sexual violation and dismemberment that drive the musical's revenge plot and second to the cannibalism of the comic plot. All of the songbirds Johanna mentions – green finches, linnet birds, nightingales, blackbirds, ringdoves, robinets and larks – point towards resonances richer than their mere ability to sing. They direct us, in fact, to the complexity of melodrama itself, which is generically difficult to define just as *we our-selves are difficult to define*. As Jonathan Goldberg argues in his recent, beautiful study of the genre, melodrama is not about stark divisions of good and evil but about the recognition that no one is just one thing. Melodrama, in its articulation of contradictions, describes the incoherence of identity within our very selves. For Goldberg, 'Home is separateness, within yourself, where you live with another, your stranger self. Coupling is impossible because no one is single, each one is divided'.[43] Melodrama sings this division.

But are Johanna's birds even singing? Johanna herself isn't actually sure. 'Are you discussing or fussing / Or simply dreaming?', she asks, 'Are you crowing? / Are you screaming?' (24). Johanna hears a dream of love and freedom in the song of the birds, but she also hears terror, and we will turn next to the screams our ingénue hears and the violence they signal.

Notes

1 Harold Clurman, reviews of *Sweeney Todd* and *Strangers*, *Nation*, 24 March 1979, 315–316.

2 Munk 85.

3 Stanley Kauffmann, "Slay It with Music," *New Republic*, 24 March 1979, 24.

4 James Fenton, "The Barberous Crimes of Sondheim and Prince," *Sunday Times* (London), 6 July 1980, 40.

5 Michael Feingold, "Sondheim, Bloody Sondheim," *Village Voice*, 15 March 1979, 85.

6 John Lahr, "Sondheim's Little Deaths: the Ironic Mode and Its Discontents," *Harper's* 258, no. 4 (1979): 78.

7 Barnes 29.

8 Julius Novick, "Sondheim, Bloody Sondheim," *Village Voice*, 12 March 1979, 85.

9   Rex Reed, "Sweeney Soars," *Daily News*, 4 March 1979, 7.

10 John Lahr, *Joy Ride: Show People and Their Shows* (New York: Norton, 2015), 362, 396.

11 John Simon, "A Little Knife Music," *New York* [magazine], 19 March 1979, 74, 75.

12 Walter Kerr, "Is Sweeney on Target?" *New York Times*, 11 March 1979, D6.

13 Martyn Sutton, "How to Write a Musical without Big Numbers," *Sunday Times* (London), 6 July 1980, 40.

14 Sondheim, *Finishing the Hat*, 332.

15 See Banfield, *Sondheim's Broadway Musicals*; and Blyton.

16 Joanne Gordon, *Art Isn't Easy: the Achievement of Stephen Sondheim* (Carbondale: Southern Illinois University Press, 1990), 214, 249.

17 William Arrowsmith, "Introduction to the *Bacchae*," in *Euripides V*, edited by David Grene and Richmond Lattimore (Chicago: University of Chicago Press, 1959) 149. See also Bernard Williams, *Shame and Necessity* (Berkeley: University of California Press, 1993), 103–167.

18 John Webster, *The Duchess of Malfi*, edited by Leah S. Marcus (London: Arden, 2009), 1.1.67–69.

19 Thomas Middleton, *The Revenger's Tragedy*, edited by MacDonald P. Jackson, in *Thomas Middleton: the Collected Works*, edited by Gary Taylor and John Lavagnino (Oxford: Clarendon, 2007), 1.1.94–95.

20 Una Ellis-Fermor, *The Jacobean Drama*, 5th edn (London: Methuen, 1965), 17–25.

21 Blyton 19; Gordon 208.

22 Richard J. Hand and Michael Wilson, *Grand-Guignol: the French Theatre of Horror* (Exeter: University of Exeter Press, 2002), 5.

23 Hand and Wilson 5.

24 Hand and Wilson 6.

25 Knapp 333.

26 Gordon 253.

27 Bertolt Brecht, "The Modern Theatre Is the Epic Theatre," translated by John Willett, in *Brecht on Theatre: the Development of*

an Aesthetic, edited by John Willett (New York: Hill and Wang, 1964), 36.

28 See Blyton 20; Kauffmann 24; and Bill Zakariasen, "*Sweeney* Returns Opera to Its Roots," *Daily News* (New York), 4 June 1979, 25.

29 Brecht 36–37.

30 Martin Gottfried, *Balancing Act: the Authorized Biography of Angela Lansbury* (Boston: Little, Brown and Company, 1999), 245.

31 Daniel C. Gerould, "Preface," *New York Literary Forum* 7 (1980): ix.

32 Sondheim, *Finishing the Hat*, 312.

33 Stephen Sondheim, "Larger than Life: Reflections on Melodrama and Sweeney Todd," *New York Literary Forum* 7 (1980): 3–14.

34 Carol Ilson, *Harold Prince: a Director's Journey*, 2nd edn (New York: Limelight, 2000), 286.

35 Foster Hirsch, *Harold Prince and the American Musical Theatre*, 2nd edn (New York: Applause, 2005), 123.

36 Thomas Hardy, "The Blinded Bird," in *The Poetical Works of Thomas Hardy Vol. 1: Collected Poems, Lyrical, Narratory, and Reflective* (London: MacMillan and Co., 1919), 418–419.

37 Mack, *Wonderful*, 171.

38 Harry Wallop, "Why French Chefs Want Us to Eat This Bird – Head, Bones, Beak and All," 18 September 2014, www.telegraph. co.uk/foodanddrink/11102100/Why-French-chefs-want-us-to-eat-this-bird-head-bones-beak-and-all.html (1 February 2018).

39 James George Frazer, *Taboo and the Perils of the Soul*, 3rd edn (New York: St Martin's Press, 1911), 116–119.

40 Malcolm Arnold, *Sweeney Todd: Ballet for Orchestra, Op. 68* (London: Faber Music, 1989), 207.

41 Stephen Sondheim, *Sweeney Todd: the Demon Barber of Fleet Street* [Score] (New York: Rilting Music, 1999), 61.

42 Ovid, *Metamorphoses*, translated by Stanley Lombardo (Indianapolis: Hackett Publishing, 2010), 6.774–776.

43 Jonathan Goldberg, *Melodrama: an Aesthetics of Impossibility* (Durham: Duke University Press, 2016), 52.

3

The throat that bleeds

Up until the show's finale, when he murders the Beggar Woman and Mrs Lovett and nearly kills his daughter, Sweeney the serial killer only 'shaves the faces of gentlemen' (1). The list of people filling the imaginary pies in 'A Little Priest' is also entirely male. *Sweeney Todd*, it would seem, is primarily interested in violence committed by men against other men. I want to begin, however, by focusing on acts of violence against the women in *Sweeney*. Acts of gendered violence – against Sweeney's wife and daughter – are the nominal motivation behind Sweeney's killing spree in the first place, and Sondheim and Wheeler's treatment of this violence deserves our attention. The title of this chapter promises a discussion of throat slashing, sadism and brutality. It will also address the pleasure the audience is asked to experience as we watch our demon barber get the revenge he seeks. But let's begin, first, with Lucy and Johanna Barker and *Sweeney*'s treatment of sexual violence.

The lecherous Judge Turpin, intent on having sex with Benjamin Barker's wife, Lucy, uses his power as a government official to bring it about. The musical describes this sexual violence in language typical of the 1800s. Sweeney tells Anthony that the Judge, after sending Barker to Australia, believed that 'there was nothing but to wait / And she would fall' (10). Anthony responds using the very same language of seduction: 'And the lady, sir – did she – succumb?' (10). In this nineteenth-century way of thinking about heterosexuality and consent, the woman does not *desire* anything from the man but somehow *gives in*, succumbs – out of poverty and not out of her own sexual desire – to the sexual desires of the man.

Mrs Lovett, that eminently practical capitalist, understands Lucy Barker's situation in precisely the same way. Lucy, she tells us, 'had her chance for the moon on a string' but 'wouldn't budge' and refused to 'use her head' (15–16). Mrs Lovett understands that a sexual relationship with Judge Turpin would reap financial benefits, and so she thinks Lucy a fool for choosing instead to be a 'poor thing' (15). Her repeated use of the word *poor* in 'Poor Thing' is intended, of course, as pitying mockery of Lucy, but the word also reminds us that penury is the worst fate – and harshest insult – Mrs Lovett can imagine. Mrs Lovett's way of thinking also reflects *legal* understandings of consent in the late nineteenth century. In her important study *Consent*, historian Pamela Haag describes the way in which individual freedom in the nineteenth century came to be understood in terms of property, through a discourse that defined freedom as the ability to engage in contractual relationships. This way of thinking 'converted consent itself into a coin of exchange, relinquished in a morally transgressive *but* freely chosen pact'.[1] Women's consent, according to this ideology, was a thing to be traded in the marketplace in exchange for monetary compensation, and Lucy's refusal to use sexual consent in this way makes her poor in both senses of the word.

Not that Lucy *does* 'succumb' or 'fall' or 'consent'. Judge Turpin brutally rapes Lucy, and, although Mrs Lovett does not describe the rape using the language of violence – instead saying euphemistically that 'She wasn't no match for such craft' – the Judge violates Lucy in full view of *Sweeney*'s audience (18). Sondheim and Wheeler's stage directions describe the violence as follows: '*the* JUDGE *appears, tears off his mask, then his cloak, revealing himself naked. She screams as he reaches for her, struggling wildly as the* BEADLE *hurls her to the floor. He holds her there as the* JUDGE *mounts her*' (17). In other words, although many of the play's nineteenth-century characters might understand rape as something to which a woman might 'succumb', *Sweeney* asks us to treat the actions of the Judge and the Beadle as rape, sexual violence enacted on the body of a woman who wants nothing to do with either of them sexually.

That Judge Turpin is first and foremost a *rapist* is essential to the Johanna–Anthony plot of *Sweeney Todd*. The Judge 'proposes' marriage to Johanna, but the audience knows that to Judge Turpin a woman's consent is merely a cover for his own sexual satisfaction. He may ask a woman for her consent, but she cannot actually refuse. If she does not consent, then, as the audience has already seen, the Judge will rape/marry her anyway. Consent matters little to the Judge if he desires a woman sexually. I say 'woman', but the Beggar Woman hints to Anthony that the Judge's sexual sadism includes a taste for young men as well as women (27). In his screenplay for the 2007 film, John Logan makes this explicit when the Judge includes 'the catamites of Greece' in his list of the pornography he enjoys.[2] This is the lecherous, violent and corrupt man whom Sweeney plans to kill. *Sweeney Todd* contains no sympathy at all for Judge Turpin; he is an unredeemed and unredeemable villain, and Sondheim and Wheeler expect us to find his murder satisfying and pleasurable.

As I noted earlier, however, violence as such is not *always* intended as a source of pleasure in *Sweeney Todd*. If we are supposed to enjoy Sweeney's murders of the Beadle, the Judge and perhaps even Pirelli or the nameless victims whom Sweeney dispatches so coldly during the second act's 'Johanna' sequence, Sondheim and Wheeler do not expect us to take pleasure in the Judge's violation of Lucy. On the contrary, they stage her anguish as 'she screams' and 'struggles wildly'. We are often asked to react with horror to the violence in *Sweeney*. Moreover, Sondheim and Wheeler often use violence specifically directed against the bodies of women to provoke the audience to fear or disgust rather than pleasure. Consider the differences in the final sequence between Sweeney's murders – in rapid succession – of the Beadle, the Beggar Woman, the Judge and Mrs Lovett. It is much easier to feel pleasurable satisfaction with the acts of violence directed at men than it is with those directed towards women. This is surely no accident.

Still, the Judge's death is well deserved, and this is essential for a revenge narrative to work. The audience might not ethically agree with a character's decision or desire to enact retribution, but we must believe the victim of that vengeance deserves his or her fate. And if the story is functioning properly, we will also *enjoy* that vengeance. Revenge is sweet, as everybody knows, but for what precisely is Sweeney getting vengeance? What justifies Sweeney's violence and allows the audience to take pleasure in the vengeance he enacts?

The audience has seen Judge Turpin rape Lucy, and so Sweeney's revenge against him is dramaturgically justified.

But in his first scene with Mrs Lovett, Sweeney himself describes his situation thus:

> Fifteen years sweating in a living hell on a trumped up charge. Fifteen years dreaming that, perhaps, I might come home to a loving wife and child. [...] Let them quake in their boots – Judge Turpin and the Beadle – for their hour has come. (19)

Sweeney, at least initially, describes his desire for revenge in terms of the damage done to *himself*, not to his wife and child. Mrs Lovett replies to Sweeney's threats with incredulous derision: 'You're going to – get 'em? You? A bleeding little nobody of a runaway convict? Don't make me laugh. You'll never get His 'igh and Mightiness! Nor the Beadle neither. Not in a million years' (19–20). Mrs Lovett understands the issue as a problem with Sweeney *himself*; he is neither rich enough nor powerful enough to be a threat to the connected and wealthy Judge Turpin. Sweeney Todd is 'a bleeding little nobody'.

Both Sondheim and Hal Prince have said repeatedly in interviews that, although the composer saw Sweeney as a man obsessed by revenge,[3] the director had more trouble understanding the show's violence – that is, until '[he] began to think of Sweeney's revenge as being against the class system that Judge Turpin represents'.[4] For Prince, *Sweeney* is in large part about the Industrial Revolution and the way in which the monotonous repetition and assembly lines of factory work dehumanize people: 'we could say that from the day the Industrial Revolution entered our lives, the conveyor belt pulled us further and further from harmony, from humanity, from nature'.[5] Prince, following Marx, describes the Industrial

Revolution as separating human beings from the land and from themselves as productive human beings.

The Industrial Revolution also attempted to turn human beings into machines, as so much labour to be converted into capital. This transformation of men into money is, of course, one of the chief concerns of *Sweeney*'s pie-making plot as a whole, but it also serves as an explanation for Sweeney's own violence. People go to work in factories, certainly, but historians have long argued that factories also go to work on people, shaping them and producing them according to the needs of industry. For historian Michel Foucault, this period of time marks a moment when the human body entered into a relationship with machinery, a dynamic in which 'the mechanism itself makes [the body] more obedient as it becomes more useful, and conversely' more useful the more obedient it becomes.[6] In *Discipline and Punish*, Foucault describes this relationship as follows:

> The human body was entering a machinery of power that explores it, breaks it down and rearranges it. A 'political anatomy', which was also a 'mechanics of power', was being born; it defined how one may have a hold over others' bodies, not only so that they may do what one wishes, but so that they may operate as one wishes, with the techniques, the speed and the efficiency that one determines. Thus discipline produces subjected and practised bodies, 'docile' bodies. Discipline increases the forces of the body (in economic terms of utility) and diminishes these same forces (in political terms of obedience).[7]

The factory literally shapes the bodies of those who labour within it – just as the prison and the asylum mould the bodies of those they incarcerate – using what Foucault calls here 'discipline' or a mechanics of power. For Foucault this disciplinary mechanics went to work on bodies long before people were old enough to work in factories or be incarcerated in prisons. It was already subjecting and disciplining bodies in primary schools, churches, hospitals, technical schools and military organizations: an enormous industrialized machine making bodies 'practised' and docile.

Reflecting Prince's emphasis on industry, the original scenic design for *Sweeney* was an enormous factory conceived by Eugene Lee. Lee's scenery dominated the stage of the nearly 2000-seat Uris Theatre for the original production, and Jack Kroll described the set as

> a huge, vaulted shed crossed by catwalks and filled chockablock with the whirring, clanking wheels, belts and ratchets of Victorian machinery. […] The effect of this monstrously beautiful setting is to body forth the Industrial Revolution. It's a portentous, ambiguous edifice – part cathedral, part factory, part prison – that dwarfs and degrades the swarming denizens of the lower orders.[8]

That Kroll saw a prison as well as a factory in the design is no accident. According to Foster Hirsch, Prince and Lee based the design on a large chamber inside Kilmainham Gaol in Dublin, which 'has a huge vaulted ceiling made out of smoked glass. In the middle of the room there is a high staircase from which a bridge, three stories high, spans the room'.[9] The factory, the church, the asylum and the prison overlap in Prince's concept and Lee's design just as they do in the system of disciplinary power described by Foucault.

The link here, between the Industrial Revolution, disciplinary power and Sweeney himself, is violence: 'Whenever Prince was asked what was made in the show's factory setting (and he was frequently asked because the story had nothing to do with factories), he would reply, "They make Sweeney Todds"'.[10] (This exchange is confusingly misconstrued and misquoted by Hirsch.[11]) The factory setting works in *Sweeney* because the factory lies just beneath the surface of literally all of industrialized life, shaping and disciplining the bodies in the city. The factory *creates* Sweeney Todd and others like him. Prince has said that

> the unifying emotion for the entire company is shared impotence. Now, obviously Sweeney's is the most dramatic, to justify all those murders. Obviously all those other people who don't see the sky except through filthy soot-covered glass would not justify mass murder, but in fact they all suffer from the same kind of impotence, which then creates rage, and rage is what is expressed most by Sweeney's behavior.[12]

Prince sees Sweeney's violence and rage not as an aberrant threat to his society but as a *product* of it.

Prince's understanding of Sweeney's violence corresponds to the work of the psychologist Erich Fromm, whose influential theories of human aggression shaped the field of violence studies in the early 1970s. In Fromm's conception of aggression, the violent person commits his act of violence in order to remake his own body, to *become* someone again. He is violent because of a need to reassure himself that he exists by being able to *do* something, a need which, in some people, is 'satisfied by having power *over* others, by experiencing their fear, by the murderer's watching the anguish in the face of his victim'.[13] The aggressor 'reassure[s] himself that he *is*' by destroying something apart from himself, proving to himself that he has the power to have an effect on something outside himself.

Fromm believed that, because of industrialization, 'modern mass man is isolated and lonely, even though he is part of a crowd; he has no convictions he could share with others, only slogans and ideologies he gets from communications media'.[14] He argued that 'aggressiveness is to be understood as part of the *social character*, not as an isolated behavior trait'.[15] Sweeney's violence and aggression, in other words, are – as Prince claims – extreme but logical outgrowths of the power-lessness, disconnection and anomie that define life in the industrialized city.

Sondheim and Wheeler indicate this powerlessness or physical weakness in Sweeney very early in the play, and the characters describe Sweeney's body as one that is dismembered and then reconstituted (or re-membered, if you prefer) over the course of the musical. At the same time as Mrs Lovett is taking apart the corpses of Sweeney's victims, Sweeney himself is proving that he is able to affect something, *he is becoming a self again* through his acts of violence.

The chorus initially describes Sweeney, in 'The Ballad of Sweeney Todd', as having pale skin and an odd eye (1). In the 'Ballad' the chorus also describes him as 'smooth' and 'subtle', 'Quick and quiet and clean' (3). I want to make a distinc-tion, however, between the narrative frame of the 'Ballad' and the Sweeney we actually meet in the flesh. I will argue in the next chapter that the differences between the Sweeney in the 'Ballad' and the one inside the story proper are the-matically important, but, for now, let us simply bracket off the ballad and address the Sweeney we see in front of our eyes.

From the first, we meet Sweeney as a weak man, one whose life has needed saving. When Anthony found him, we are told, Sweeney had been 'pitching and tossing on [a] raft' at sea (6). It is true that in the next scene Mrs Lovett refers to Benjamin Barker as 'beautiful' (15), but this attribution remains firmly in the past tense, and Sweeney has been so physically altered by the circumstances of his imprisonment and shipwreck that Mrs Lovett apparently has trouble recognizing him and exclaims 'So changed! Good God, what did they do to you down there in bloody Australia or wherever?' (18). As I have already noted, Mrs Lovett also refers to Sweeney as 'a bleeding little nobody', but it is Todd himself who indicates to the audience that his body is *incomplete* when he holds up his razor at the end of 'My Friends' and says 'My right arm is complete again!' (22). His arm may be complete, but we later find in 'Epiphany' a man whose psyche has fractured: Sondheim calls him 'schizophrenic'.[16] He is 'alive at last' but unable to craft a coherent identity out of the selves he contains (96). 'Epiphany', not surprisingly, is the song in which Sweeney decides to murder everyone in the world; Sondheim and Wheeler stage, in other words, the way in which rejecting one's own brokenness can generate aggression.

Prince's idea of the factory that produces Sweeney Todds, though, demands that nearly *all* of the characters in the musical appear incomplete or missing some part of themselves. For Prince, Sweeney is only an extreme version of the anomie experienced by all in society; the musical accordingly imagines a majority of its characters as dismembered or broken, working to put themselves back together. In act two, Anthony repeats the image of the right arm as separate from the body, telling Johanna 'I trust [Mr. Todd] as I trust my right arm' (172). This dismembered arm–hand imagery is introduced by Sweeney in his first song when he describes the Judge as a disembodied 'claw' (10); it is maintained by Pirelli's seemingly detached hand which, in a brief, farcical interlude, flails wildly in an attempt to attract Tobias's attention (65–66); and it is extended when Anthony asks Johanna to 'Favor me, favor me / With your hand' (73).

Most of *Sweeney*'s characters are missing something mentally as well as physically. The Beggar Woman refers to her own 'wanderin' wits' in the play's first scene and then describes herself in pieces, inviting Anthony to 'push me crumpet' and 'fish me squiff' (7). In 'The Worst Pies in London', Mrs Lovett describes herself as 'A woman alone / With limited wind' (14) and later calls herself 'cracked in the head' (20). And when Anthony first sees Johanna from afar, he finds himself in love not with *her* so much as with her yellow hair, a portion easily separable from the woman herself (31). Indeed, in act two Anthony will discuss purchasing *only* Johanna's hair from Mr Fogg (166).

Little Tobias, when he introduces himself, is attempting to convince the crowd that he, too, is missing part of his body, a part which grew back when he took Pirelli's Miracle Elixir. At least one woman in the crowd thinks Tobias is talking about his penis; he isn't, but the link to impotence here is thematic as well as humorous (34). And while we're on the subject of genitals, Judge Turpin, in his lecherous song, refers to his own penis as a thing separate from himself – 'this / Hot / Red / Devil' – and contrasts it with yet another piece of Johanna, this time her 'Soft / White / Cool / Virgin / Palms' (196). The link between violence and sexual parts is made even more literal by Mrs Lovett in 'By the Sea' when she tells Sweeney that he could 'Bring along [his] chopper' (140); Sondheim gleefully points out that '"chopper" is British slang for penis'.[17] For Joseph Marchesani, *Sweeney*'s 'razors also operate as a negative Phallus, evoking the threat of emasculation, the castration anxiety of a thwarted or lost sexuality'.[18] We are speaking of body parts, in other words, that also threaten to break apart the bodies of others, and the play slips between these meanings easily.

Sweeney Todd turns our attention to the self as something wounded, fractured or broken. Sondheim and Wheeler serve us their characters in pieces – even the ones who have not yet been butchered and turned into pie filling – and the characters work to become unified selves; they attempt to make those pieces into something whole. But this effort is always futile. The body's borders can never be made completely secure, as Julia Kristeva tells us in *Powers of Horror*. Rather, we find our selves – we define the borders of the self – in a continuous process of separating the self from that which is dead. We mark the 'I' as distinct from dead hair, extracted teeth, dead skin, fingernails, excrement – the pieces that fall (*cadere*) off the body and become non-human, the non-self. We see these rejected parts of ourselves as some-thing else, something abject, while we see ourselves as alive. Kristeva says

> There, I am at the border of my condition as a living being. My body extricates itself, as being alive, from that border. Such wastes drop so that I might live, until, from loss to loss, nothing remains in me and my entire body falls beyond the limit – *cadere*, cadaver.[19]

In *Sweeney* this process of abjection and horror is clearest onstage when we watch Tobias greedily eat pies after he has been locked in the bakehouse at the end of act two. This happens at the same time as Sweeney is slitting the Beadle's throat. The stage directions read as follows: '*In the bakehouse,*

TOBIAS *stands by the grinding machine eating a pie. He feels something on his tongue, puts a finger in his mouth and pulls the something out, holding it up for inspection*' (161–162). Tobias has found a long black hair. He decides that it cannot be one of Mrs Lovett's but thinks nothing of it and, therefore, '*He continues to eat. He bites on something else, takes it out of his mouth, looks at it*' (162). This second non-food item is a 'bit of fingernail', and once Tobias finds this he (quite understandably) gives up eating and drops the pie.

The sequence is intended as a kind of mixed, horrific pleasure for the audience. *We are waiting* for Toby to find out the truth about Mrs Lovett's pies, and so we watch with satisfied – dare I say pleasant – revulsion as Toby finds the human remains there. Both this discovery sequence and the actual items Tobias discovers in his mouth are traditional. In Dibdin Pitt's *String of Pearls*, the young baker Jarvis is eating pies when he finds a long hair and then: 'A bone? No; a button! I don't think I like pies now'.[20] As Brian Burton updated the sequence for *Sweeney Todd the Barber* in 1962, Jarvis first found a hair and then: 'What's this – a bone? No, a toe nail! How did a toe nail come into a pie? I don't think I like pies now'.[21] In Burton's version, the character immediately begins to retch and cry out in agony.

The same distasteful sequence, then, has been thrilling and disgusting theatre audiences for a century and a half. Directors of *Sweeney* after Prince have even occasionally invented new and interesting ways to stage this abjection. For the Royal National Theatre production in London in 1993, Declan Donnellan had Julia McKenzie's Mrs Lovett literally empty a pail of blood onto the stage, an image that Sondheim says he sometimes thinks about when he needs to 'remind [him]self of what musical theater can be'.[22]

I have been moving, in this chapter, from describing Sweeney's efforts to affect the world as a way to combat the powerlessness and disunity he feels, to the tendency of *all* of *Sweeney*'s characters to see themselves as incomplete or in pieces, to describing the audience's pleasure and revulsion at watching this dismemberment or disunity. If the characters see themselves as incomplete, it is important for us to note that we, too, struggle to see ourselves as whole. For an audience, part of the pleasurable effect of watching Tobias fish a fingernail out of his mouth or seeing Mrs Lovett dump a bucket of blood down a drain is a kind of Kristevan reassurance for ourselves *that we are alive*, that we are not in pieces, that we possess a self that is coherent and cohesive. Because we, like Sweeney and the other characters in the musical, frequently experience ourselves as incoherent or incomplete, this feeling of wholeness or identity creates pleasure for the audience.

In order to bring to a close this discussion of violence and dismemberment in *Sweeney*, I want to address another, only slightly different, set of audience responses that has frequently accompanied the musical. In April 2016, the *Guardian* and CNN both reported a curious story from Auckland, New Zealand. During a production of *Sweeney* at Saint Kentigern College, two 16-year-old boys actually had their throats cut (without fatality) by the teenage actor playing the demon barber. According to an investigation conducted after the incident, the drama department at the school was found to have been using actual razors as properties in the show! The boys were both hospitalized with neck injuries but released the following day, and the show went on after the cancellation of only a single performance.

Intriguingly, the authors of news descriptions of these accidental acts of violence (simultaneously theatrical and real) seemed to take a perverse pleasure in their reportage, detailing the exact condition of the razor, noting acidly that 'The school's promotional materials for its production featured an image of a bloodied straight razor resting on a pie', and then going on to recount other injuries in different theatres and other harm accidentally inflicted on the bodies of unsuspecting performers. CNN, for example, closed its piece on the injuries by saying that

> In January, an Italian actor was killed in a botched hanging scene in an experimental theater performance in Pisa, and the following month a Japanese actor died when he was stabbed in the stomach with a samurai sword during rehearsal.[23]

The *Guardian*'s version of the New Zealand story includes a link to an op-ed entitled 'Slitting Your Throat and Other Theatrical Hazards', in which the author, Michael Simkins, opines that 'Stages are dangerous places' and goes on to recount a litany of anecdotes about accidents and mishaps that he's heard over many years.[24]

These news items, while appearing conscientiously to report the failings of the safety systems in place in these theatres, mask a barely concealed hostility towards the performers they discuss. Simkins even describes his own feelings about 'The news that actor Daniel Hoevels accidentally slit his own throat on stage in Austria during a performance of *Mary Stuart*' as 'empathy mixed with schadenfreude'. Compare these reports with Craig Zadan's discussion of some 'preview difficulties' that *Sweeney*'s original production had before opening at the Uris:

'The big problem is – how to make the blood spout properly from the victims' freshly slit throats,' reported the 'Page Six' gossip column in the *New York Post* on February 19, 1979. 'Angela Lansbury and Len Cariou are feeling lucky. They barely escaped getting hit and possibly injured when a heavy bridge fell inches from them on stage,' reported Earl Wilson in the February 26, 1979, edition of the same paper.[25]

Writers for the *Post* and other newspapers seemed to take delight in reporting the show's troubles. 'It was awful', said Sondheim of this period of preview rehearsals. 'I hated it because all the professional bitches come to the first preview and tell their friends how terrible it is'.[26] Whether Sondheim imagined this hostility or not, it is certainly fair to say that, while these news media seemed to take a moral position that condemned the theatre in general – and *Sweeney Todd* in particular – for staging violent spectacles and for 'mak[ing] a profit in exploiting pain', as John Lahr put it, they also trafficked in sadism themselves.[27] A description of a close shave with murderous scenery is, in fact, a rather transparent attempt to replicate the very pleasures *Sweeney* promises.

Stephen Banfield comes close to describing the violent pleasures of theatre-going when he says that 'live theater, especially in a piece such as *Sweeney Todd*, is in any case a kind of S and M contract, actors and technicians having to submit to, command, and trust each other in deadly earnest if a performance is to come off without lethal mishap'.[28] The erotically charged pleasures of S/M seem to me an odd frame for thinking about stage technicians and performers (theirs is essentially a relationship of labourers working together), but it is perhaps an excellent way to think about the relationship between the *audience* and the performers onstage.[29]

Sweeney Todd, it is true, is in the business of cultivating audiences who enjoy watching acts of brutality, witnessing slashed throats and chuckling while unsuspecting diners gobble down pies filled with minced human flesh. But Sondheim and Wheeler's melodrama also takes pains to point out the causes of that violence, and the show's cannibalism (as we will see in the next chapter) is designed as a provocation and a point of discussion, not merely a disgusting plot twist. What these news-media reports make clear is that audiences and critics, whether they're watching *Sweeney Todd* or not, are, at least in part, out for blood.

Sondheim and Wheeler only rarely eroticize the violence in *Sweeney Todd*. The relationship that the show creates between sexual desire and violence is complex and intriguing, but the story I've been telling in this chapter is one in which audience members attend a tale of dismemberment and violence and are asked in turn to recognize both the violence of their own societies and the incoherence of their own selves. *Sweeney*'s audiences are not simply permitted to enjoy the sadistic pleasure of witnessing a set of fictional murders.

Lahr may, after all, be correct when he claims witheringly that 'The theme of the dead heart trying to resuscitate itself dominates much of Sondheim's work', but that theme is essentially a hopeful one, and the critic's position that *Sweeney* portrays 'a world where evil holds no odium and life no significance' is an untenable one.[30] *Sweeney Todd* asks us to enjoy violence, but it does not ask that we accept corruption without protest, and it does not reduce evil to a banality. Sweeney himself may complain that 'the cruelty of men / Is as wondrous as Peru', but the show in which

Sweeney stars does not serve us that cruelty as something that can be enjoyed or consumed without consequence (9). Pleasure in *Sweeney Todd* never goes down easily, and evil tastes bitter on the tongue.

Taste, as it happens, is the subject of our next chapter, which will begin with a discussion of *sexual* tastes and then transition to the atrocity of cannibalism that is the musical's essential subject matter.

Notes

1 Pamela Haag, *Consent: Sexual Rights and the Transformation of American Liberalism* (Ithaca: Cornell University Press, 1999), 34.

2 John Logan, *Sweeney Todd: the Demon Barber of Fleet Street*, 2006, www.joblo.com/scripts/script_sweeneytodd.pdf (accessed 15 July 2017), 23.

3 Gretchen Cryer, "On Collaboration between Authors and Directors," *Dramatists Guild Quarterly* 16, no. 2 (1979): 14.

4 Hirsch 120.

5 Hirsch 120.

6 Michel Foucault, *Discipline and Punish: the Birth of the Prison*, translated by Alan Sheridan (New York: Vintage, 1979), 138.

7 Foucault 138.

8 Jack Kroll, "The Blood Runs Cold," *Newsweek*, 12 March 1979, 101.

9 Hirsch 120.

10 Martin Gottfried, *Sondheim*, 2nd edn (New York: Harry N. Abrams, 2000), 127.

11 Hirsch 129.

12 Cryer 14.

13 Erich Fromm, *The Anatomy of Human Destructiveness* (New York: Holt, Rinehart and Winston, 1973), 236.

14 Fromm 107.

15 Fromm 167.

16   Horowitz 140.

17   Sondheim, *Finishing the Hat*, 368.

18   Joseph Marchesani, "Arresting Development: Law, Love, and the Name-of-the-Father in *Sweeney Todd*," in *Reading Stephen Sondheim*, edited by Sandor Goodhart (New York: Garland, 2000), 176.

19   Julia Kristeva, *Powers of Horror: an Essay on Abjection*, translated by Leon S. Roudiez (New York: Columbia University Press, 1982), 3.

20   Dibdin Pitt 253.

21   Burton 32.

22   Stephen Sondheim, *Look, I Made a Hat: Collected Lyrics (1981–2011) with Attendant Comments, Amplifications, Dogmas, Harangues, Digressions, Anecdotes and Miscellany* (New York: Knopf, 2011), xx.

23   Tim Hume, "Teen Actors' Necks Slit in School Production of *Sweeney Todd*," 8 April 2016, www.cnn.com/2016/04/07/asia/new-zealand-sweeney-todd-razor/index.html (accessed 1st February 2018).

24   Michael Simkins, "Slitting Your Throat and Other Theatrical Hazards," 11 December 2008, www.theguardian.com/stage/theatreblog/2008/dec/11/theatre-slit-throat-austrian-actor (1 February 2018).

25   Craig Zadan, *Sondheim & Co.*, 2nd edn (New York: Harper & Row, 1989), 255.

26   Zadan 255.

27   Lahr, "Sondheim's Little Deaths," 74.

28   Banfield, "Sondheim's Genius," 16.

29   See also Leo Bersani and Ulysse Dutoit, *Forms of Violence: Narrative in Assyrian Art and Modern Culture* (New York: Schocken Books, 1985), 37–39.

30   Lahr, "Sondheim's Little Deaths," 74, 78.

4

The throat that swallows

With a musical as interested in violence and bloodshed as *Sweeney*, one might expect it to eroticize violence much more than it actually does. The Judge's rape of Lucy in act one is certainly an act of sexualized violence, but as we have seen, this sequence makes a clear distinction between erotics and violence, and it focuses on the anguish experienced by Lucy, not on the pleasure the Judge takes. Another image of violent sexuality in *Sweeney* is the Judge's version of 'Johanna', in which he masturbates while flogging himself (193–196). This act of masochism, however, is informed by the rape we have already seen the Judge commit, and again Sondheim and Wheeler focus on violence rather than erotics: Judge Turpin violently lashes himself while he plots the violation of his adopted daughter. The audience is invited to take a perspective critical of the judge's actions, not one that identifies with them.

There is one more sequence in which violence and erotics are joined in the musical. Sweeney and Judge Turpin's song 'Pretty Women' is a kind of love duet between two men. They sing about their relationship with one another while seeming to sing about two (absent) women whom they both desire. The song quite clearly eroticizes violence. The men discuss women 'blowing out their candles', 'breathing lightly' and 'combing out their hair', while at the same time Sweeney holds a razor to the Judge's neck (89–90). The act of one man shaving another is certainly intimate, an act in which one man is vulnerable to another – this is one of the reasons why the Sweeney Todd legend has endured so long – and Sweeney's scene with the Judge ramps up the erotics of this vulnerability when the barber promises a shave that is 'The closest I ever gave' (86). The song is dramaturgically erotic, as well. The scene traffics in an economy of anticipatory pleasure, delaying the gratifying release for which the audience is waiting. Mrs Lovett has told Sweeney (and us) that 'Half the fun is to / Plan the plan', that 'good things come to / Those who can / Wait', and so the audience waits for violence (58). We watch with desire and anticipatory pleasure as Sweeney toys with the vulnerable Judge and they sing their song about the beauty of women. 'Pretty Women' is the most erotic song in *Sweeney Todd*, and its erotics are all violent.

This means that all of the violent sexuality in the show is related to Judge Turpin, the show's unredeemed villain. Not that *Sweeney Todd* lacks *non-violent* erotics: Mrs Lovett, the Beggar Woman, Tobias, Sweeney, Johanna and Anthony all speak quite openly about sex and desire. Even Beadle Bamford has time to state his opinion about the personal grooming habits necessary for attracting a potential sexual partner (74–75). The images of desire and sexuality associated with these characters, however, are not violent ones.

The erotics of *Sweeney Todd* are focused more frequently on images of ingestion. *Sweeney* is a show with a sexuality that is much more oral than it is genital or even manual (despite its frequent fixation on arms and hands). Very early in the play, the Beggar Woman asks Anthony to 'push me crumpet' (7), a lyric Sondheim eventually replaced with another food metaphor, 'push me parsley'.[1] But the majority of *Sweeney*'s sexual imagery comes from Mrs Lovett, whose name, you'll remember, is a holdover from a time when the character was understood as primarily motivated by lust.

Mrs Lovett's songs insist on the character as a sexual being, no matter how grotesque or disagreeable her actions. From her very first appearance Mrs Lovett surprises the audience with the vulgar double entendre 'Popping pussies into pies', and her second-act seduction song, 'By the Sea' (perhaps the musical's strangest song), is energized by both sexual desire and food imagery. The purpose of 'By the Sea' is Mrs Lovett's articulation of a fantasy in which she and Mr Todd get married and buy a house by the seaside. As the song begins, the images Mrs Lovett conjures are predominantly either sexual or gustatory and occasionally both. She imagines her lover and her together 'Underneath our flannel' (139), their 'rumpled bedding / Legitimized' (140), and she consistently refers to the pleasures of eating: she dreams of 'hav[ing] tea and scones' with Sweeney (138) or 'turn[ing] into butter' when they say 'I do' (140). Her lyric 'Every night in the kip / When we're through our kippers / I'll be there slippin' off your slippers' perfectly merges the sensual pleasures of eating and sex, giving the audience an image of desire that is sexual as well as ingestive (137). Mrs Lovett is 'so happy – / I could – / Eat you up, I really could', a phrase she says while kissing Sweeney on the lips repeatedly (136). At the end of 'By the Sea' she continues this association between sex and food, offering Sweeney a bon-bon but, in a bait-and-switch move, kissing him again instead.

At the end of act one, Mrs Lovett uses the pun on 'pussy' a second time, associating cunnilingus with pie-eating, in 'A Little Priest', a song positively stuffed with sexual meanings and double entendres (14). 'A pussy's good for maybe six or / Seven at the most', she muses, 'And I'm sure they can't compare / As far as taste' (98). Moreover, it isn't only female genitalia Mrs Lovett imagines her customers eating: she would bake and serve a general 'With or without his privates' – '"With" is extra', naturally – and she offers Sweeney 'rear admiral' (106) and 'Royal / Marine', which, she tells us suggestively, 'tastes of wherever it's been' (101). The title of 'A Little Priest' is itself a pun on genitalia, and, even when the song is not being explicit about sexual organs, Mrs Lovett is still, after all, asking the audience to take pleasure in imagining *how various men taste*, an act of intimacy whether the person in one's mouth is dead or alive.

'A Little Priest' is a song supported entirely by an erotics of ingestion. Even more intriguingly, 'A Little Priest' marks the moment in the play when Sweeney and Mrs Lovett seem to be most synchronized. They become annoyed with each other again as soon as the second act begins, but in their first-act finale Sweeney and Mrs Lovett make each other laugh, speak to each other affectionately, and finish each other's sentences. As Raymond Knapp puts it,

The most disturbing dimension of this number [...] is that it presents the first real human connection in the show, the first meshing of sensibilities within what passes for genuine community in musical terms. And we are so starved [pun intended] for that musical gesture that we embrace it despite the fact that what they are contemplating is the establishment of a factory for killing, baking, and selling human beings as food for other human beings.[2]

This delightful song, dedicated as it is to cannibalistic atrocity, is a high point for the pleasures the musical has to offer, perfectly merging the show's horror elements and its romance. *Sweeney Todd*, in fact, never really imagines erotics without also reminding us of horror – as the discussion of Johanna's birds demonstrated earlier.

Sweeney Todd is most notably a musical about murder *and* cannibalism. Melodramas are, after all, filled with scoundrels plotting evil, but it is a remarkable villain indeed who commits barbarism on the level of cannibalistic revenge. This anthropophagy, we should note, is Mrs Lovett's idea, not Sweeney's, and if our attention has been focused on her in our discussion of the show's erotics, she and her suspiciously popular meat pies will also demand our attention as we turn to the play's portrayal of cannibalism.

The theatre has been interested in cannibalism from its earliest incarnations, and the *meanings* of cannibalism in the theatre have changed a great deal over time. At least four ancient Greek poets wrote theatrical versions of the story of Tantalus, who killed and cooked his son Pelops as a banquet for the gods. No fewer than *eight* playwrights from ancient Greece – and at least another five from ancient Rome – wrote tragedies about Thyestes, the king who was tricked by his vengeful brother Atreus into feasting on his own children. Most of these plays are no longer extant, so we can make few judgments about how the playwrights used their cannibalistic subject matter to make meaning, but Seneca's *Thyestes*, which has survived, does not treat cannibalism as a metaphor. The *Thyestes* presents cannibalism as incomparable barbarism, an atrocity from which even the gods hide their faces.

The *Thyestes* would become a model for much of the Early Modern revenge tragedy discussed in Chapter 2, and Seneca's play was most notably an inspiration for William Shakespeare's cannibalistic drama *Titus Andronicus*, in which the protagonist vows revenge after suffering betrayal, dismemberment and the death of most of his sons. Late in the play's final act, Titus, whom everyone thinks is insane, captures the men who have raped and mutilated his daughter, Lavinia, and tells them what he will do to them:

> Hark, villains, I will grind your bones to dust,
> And with your blood and it I'll make a paste,
> And of the paste a coffin [pie-crust] will I rear,
> And make two pasties of your shameful heads,
> And bid that strumpet, your unhallowed dam,
> Like to the earth swallow her own increase.
> This is the feast that I have bid her to,
> And this the banquet she shall surfeit on:
> For worse than Philomel you used my daughter,
> And worse than [Procne] I will be revenged.[3]

Titus – who is by no means the play's villain – will make meat pies of his enemies and feed the young men to their mother.

Shakespeare's tragedy, which is rarely mentioned in scholarship on *Sweeney Todd*, has other similarities to Sondheim and Wheeler's play. First, although revenge appears caused by madness, in both plays it is motivated (if not justified) by rape. Second, note Shakespeare's reference to Philomela and Procne's cannibalistic revenge, also for the crime of rape.

Before committing his atrocity, Titus cites the revenge of his predecessors, a poetic gesture that places the character within a genealogy of cannibalistic revengers. The characters in *Sweeney Todd* avoid literary references as a rule – Mrs Lovett doesn't read Shakespeare or Ovid, much less Seneca or Middleton – but Sondheim and Wheeler place their characters within this cannibalistic genealogy nonetheless. I have already noted the reference to Philomela and Procne in 'Green Finch and Linnet Bird', and we might also imagine Sweeney's incomplete arm as a reference to Titus's own handless arm, dismembered by the villain Aaron in act three of Shakespeare's play.

Titus Andronicus links cannibalism to revenge in a way that is similar to *Sweeney*. As in Seneca's *Thyestes*, cannibalism in *Andronicus* is presented as an excessive, outrageous response to having been wronged; it is a poisonous meal that infects the person serving as well as the person served – both Titus and Sweeney will have to die after they've taken their revenge. But *Andronicus* and *Sweeney* differ from the *Thyestes* in their treatment of pleasure. Seneca's play is horrified by cannibalism; *Andronicus* and *Sweeney* ask the audience to enjoy it. Shakespeare presents revenge as an act in which the audience – overwhelmed by Titus's misfortunes for the play's preceding five acts – can finally take pleasure. *Sweeney* does precisely the same thing, instead placing this pleasure at the end of act one.

Still, the cannibalism in *Andronicus*, like that in the *Thyestes*, is not a metaphor for something else. It is itself – an arrogant, outrageous act of atrocity. Later in his career, however, Shakespeare returned to cannibalism. In *Timon of Athens* (co-written with Middleton), Shakespeare uses the metaphor of anthropophagy repeatedly. The image of one man devouring another runs throughout *Timon*, and it is always used in the same way. The play's malcontent character, Apemantus, sets up this imagery in a long speech in act one, complaining 'O you gods, what a number of men eats Timon and he sees 'em not! It grieves me to see so many dip their meat in one man's blood'. Apemantus then moves into iambic pentameter in order to moralize: 'I wonder men dare trust themselves with men, / Methinks they should invite them without knives – / Good for their meat and safer for their lives'.[4] When characters feast in *Timon* they gorge themselves on the blood of others.

Timon is a play about money; it is about loans and debt and theft. This is quite clearly *Sweeney Todd*'s metaphor, as well. 'For what's the sound of the world out there?' Sweeney asks. 'It's man devouring man, my dear, / And who are we / To deny it in here?' (99). Cannibalism in *Sweeney*, as in *Timon*, is a metaphor for the devaluation and exploitation of other human beings for profit. It is also a way to visualize that exploitation in material terms, whereby Sondheim and Wheeler present the idea that stealing from someone is identical to taking a pound of flesh off his or her body (as yet another Shakespeare play would have it).

Michel de Montaigne, in his essay 'Of Cannibals' (1580), made a similar criticism of civilized society, comparing the exploitation of others to the consumption of men:

> I think there is more barbarity in eating a man alive than in eating him dead; and in tearing by tortures and the rack a body still full of feeling, in roasting a man bit by bit, in having him bitten and mangled by dogs and swine (as we have not only read but seen within fresh memory, not among ancient enemies, but among neighbors and

> fellow citizens, and what is worse, on the pretext of piety
> and religion), than in roasting and eating him after he is
> dead.[5]

Montaigne was not writing in favour of cannibalism *per se*; his
aim was rather to point out that we are ourselves barbaric, and
that our society's justifications for torture and destruction are
just as bad as cannibalism. 'So we may well call these people
barbarians, in respect to the rules of reason', says Montaigne,
'but not in respect to ourselves, who surpass them in every
kind of barbarity'.[6]

As Montaigne discusses cannibalism, he moves to criticism of his own society, describing the visit of three so-called
cannibals to see Charles IX, King of France. The three men

> noticed that there were among us men full and gorged
> with all sorts of good things, and that their other halves
> were beggars at their doors, emaciated with hunger and
> poverty; and they thought it strange that these needy
> halves could endure such an injustice and did not take
> the others by the throat, or set fire to their houses.[7]

The comparison to *Sweeney* works perfectly. Sweeney and Mrs
Lovett live in a civilized society similar to the one Montaigne
describes, one which has 'two kinds of men and only two', in
which one man has 'his foot / In the other one's face' (94).
And like the city Montaigne imagines, Sweeney's city, too,
will soon be set on fire by those treated unjustly.

The use of the cannibalism metaphor in *Sweeney Todd*, then,
comes from the Renaissance – from Shakespeare, Middleton
and Montaigne. Scholars and critics, however, have more
frequently noted *Sweeney*'s debts to the work of playwright

Bertolt Brecht. Brecht's plays portray men not only *devouring* other men but also *converting them into money*, as in his teaching play *The Measures Taken* (1930). Mrs Lovett's recipe for feeding corpses to customers is, as Joanne Gordon puts it, 'the perversion of the social contract and the breakdown of all fellow feeling fittingly symbolized by the capitalistic cannibalism she proposes'.[8] David Savran and Daniel Gundlach more succinctly put it as follows: '*Sweeney Todd* remains the only musical that uses cannibalism as a metaphor for capitalist modes of production and consumption'.[9] The cannibalism in *Sweeney Todd* is, without question, a metaphor for the exploitation that the Judge and the Beadle demonstrate and Sweeney and Mrs Lovett denounce. In their pie shop, unlike everywhere else, 'those above will serve those down below!' (102). Their actions are a kind of enormous act of societal revenge – akin to setting the city on fire.

Even those who have found *Sweeney*'s central metaphor distasteful have understood it to work this way. Many critics of the show's first production took issue with the Brechtian equation of capitalism and cannibalism. A frequent criticism of *Sweeney*, as I noted in Chapter 2, was that the show managed to merge pleasure and cultural criticism. Critics seemed to labour under the mistaken impression that Brechtian theatre – theatre that is critical of capitalism and draws attention to a society's structural inequalities – isn't supposed to include fun. Take Jack Kroll's version of this common critique: 'There's Broadway in the fun and games of the meat-pie song', he complained in *Newsweek*, 'And there's Brecht in another song, which proclaims: "The history of the world, my sweet / Is who gets eaten and who gets to eat"'.[10] For Kroll, *Sweeney* doesn't successfully fuse Broadway and Brecht, even though 'the meat-pie song' and the song in which we are told that

'The history of the world [...] is who gets eaten and who gets to eat' are, in fact, the same song. But Brecht always intended his theatre to be fun; this was why he wrote so many musicals.

We will stay with both Brecht and cannibalism for a bit longer, but as we conclude I want to heed Rosalind Crone's warning in *Violent Victorians* that 'Although important, we should not dwell for too long upon the theme of industrial capitalism in "The String of Pearls". After all, it was nothing new'.[11] Crone points out that melodramas on stage as well as the penny bloods circulating among nineteenth-century readers often portrayed the exploitation of the working class by the wealthy, and these media frequently represented the way in which traditional morality had been disregarded by people more interested in amassing wealth than in alleviating the sufferings of the poor.

For Crone, what is important about *The String of Pearls* is that Sweeney and Mrs Lovett construct a finely tuned *murder machine*. Crone is interested in the way the story uses cannibalism to talk not about capitalism, but about industrial technologies. We have already discussed the way in which Prince's original production of *Sweeney* was fundamentally interested in industry and technology, but Crone's caution also reminds us that, over time, metaphors can shift meaning. Precisely because critics have found *Sweeney Todd*'s equation of cannibalism and capitalism so clear, I want to examine two other ideas that Mrs Lovett's pie shop might suggest to us – new meanings that have perhaps opened up since the show's original production.

First, several recent cannibalism narratives have used anthropophagy as a metaphor for the eating of meat in general. This theme is clearly visible in films like Julia Ducournau's *Raw* (2016) and Ana Lily Amirpour's *The Bad Batch* (2016).

Although the subject matter of these stories is the eating of *human* flesh, one of the purposes of the narratives is to ask audiences to think again about their own practices of eating *animal* flesh. In both movies, cannibalism is intended as a kind of Brechtian alienation effect: it makes the practice of eating meat seem strange or abnormal and asks us to examine the ethics of our own carnivorous consumption. This is a relatively new focus for narratives about cannibalism – we do not, for example, find this in *Andronicus* or the *Thyestes* – but it can help us to locate this theme in Sondheim and Wheeler's musical.

What, after all, is filling Mrs Lovett's pies *before* she starts stuffing them with human remains? In act one her pies are disgusting. We know this because she tells us so and because Sweeney tastes one and spits it out. Her pies apparently have no filling at all or very little filling: they're 'nothing but crusting', 'Only lard and nothing more' (13–14). Mrs Lovett suspects that her competitor, Mrs Mooney, is stuffing her pies with the neighbourhood cats, and we might dismiss this simply as slander, were it not that Mrs Lovett intimates that she would be following a similar practice if she were limber enough to trap a local feline herself. Mrs Lovett also notes that meat is very expensive, and the portrait she paints of the London meat market is a decidedly unappetizing one:

> Never
> Thought I'd live to see the day men'd think it was a
> Treat finding poor
> Animals
> Wot are dying in the street. (13–14)

Bond's play paints this image even more vividly; his Mrs Lovett says 'I never thought I'd see the day when grown men and good cooks, too, would dribble over a dead dog like it was a round of beef'.[12] Londoners in *Sweeney Todd* are willing to treat sick and dying animals as food sources.

Still more troubling, perhaps, is the sequence in which Mrs Lovett instructs Tobias about the meat grinder: 'you know the secret that makes the pies so sweet and tender? Three times. You must put the meat through the grinder three times […] Smoothly, smoothly. And as soon as a new batch of meat comes in, we'll put you to work' (155). Ground meat was often treated as suspicious or in some way tainted in sensational 'penny fiction' like the original *String of Pearls*.[13] And the human remains Tobias grinds, so happily devoured by Mrs Lovett's customers, ought surely to put audiences in mind of the processed meat we ourselves consume – sausages and chicken nuggets, taco filling and hamburgers, hot dogs and lunchmeat, shawarma and chili con carne. Honestly, it's enough to make the most committed carnivore ask for a salad.

Second, cannibalism in popular lore is frequently associated with immortality. Vampires, werewolves, zombies and other monsters who feed on human flesh often live forever because of the taboo food they consume. The dark shamans who practise *kanaimà* – a form of cannibalistic vampirism – in the Guyana highlands similarly believe that their ritual food makes them immortal.[14] In fact, one needn't go into the jungles of South America to find cannibalistic practices that promise immortality: the eternal life promised by Roman Catholicism is dependent in part upon the consumption of human flesh in the sacrament of communion. Mrs Lovett's unsuspecting customers will not, of course, live forever because of her pies. But immortality cannot be dismissed so quickly as we consider *Sweeney*, for Sweeney Todd – whose name in German actually *means* death – does not, in fact, die. Or, rather, *he has already died*. He rises from the grave at the beginning of the musical, has his throat slit by Tobias, and then rises from the grave again at the show's end. It seems rather obvious when put this way, but Sweeney, like a vampire or zombie, is plainly one of the undead.

Sweeney has long been associated with the supernatural or metaphysical, and these demonic associations are described repeatedly by the ensemble. We are told that 'Sweeney heard music that nobody heard', that 'He served a dark and a vengeful god' (3). The chorus tells us that he kills 'To satisfy the hungry god / Of Sweeney Todd' (164), and the show ends with the phrase 'To seek revenge may lead to hell, / But everyone does it, and seldom as well' (191). Sweeney is associated in these lyrics with the powers of the underworld and with evil divinities. He is himself a demon, and the chorus is unwavering on this point.[15] These associations are traditional. Crone dates the link between Sweeney and the underworld from 1878, when the story's title added a word: 'Todd became the *Demon Barber of Fleet Street*. But most telling was the new attention given to the abnormalities and even supernatural occurrences surrounding his birth and childhood'.[16] In many of the Sweeney Todd plays that precede Sondheim and Wheeler's, Sweeney seems insane, demonic, and occasionally appears to possess superhuman strength or a Svengali-like ability to persuade other characters to do things.

Sweeney's resurrections, on the other hand, are Sondheim and Wheeler's invention. Sweeney does not appear as undead in Bond's play or in any of the previous versions of the tale. Further, the resurrections are contained within another of the musical's unique contributions to the Sweeney story, 'The Ballad of Sweeney Todd' itself. The 'Ballad' is more than a narrative frame; it exists outside of the time of the play itself, commenting on the play and interrupting Sweeney's story. The 'Ballad' calls the story into being. The phrase 'Attend the tale of Sweeney Todd' announces that Sweeney's story will happen; the 'Ballad' *makes* the story happen (1). It is *outside* of the story proper that Sweeney returns from the dead and begins to tell us his own story, and it is in the show's epilogue – again within the 'Ballad' – that Sweeney rises from the grave the second time.

There are, indeed, some important differences between the 'Ballad' and the play itself. What the 'Ballad' tells us we are going to see is not exactly what the musical shows to the audience. Sweeney's shop, for example, does not have 'fancy clients and good renown' (2). 'His room [is] bare', certainly, but could we call the Sweeney we meet in the play 'subtle' or 'Inconspicuous' or 'Quick and quiet and clean' (2–3)? We might, but it would surely be a stretch. And is it really true that 'He seldom laughed but he often smiled' as the chorus says (23)? The Sweeney of the 'Ballad', in other words, isn't quite the Sweeney we meet inside the musical. On the contrary, the 'Ballad' describes the Sweeney of legend, the Sweeney who sends rats scuttling with a glance, who threatens to cut Tobias's throat from ear to ear. The lyrics of the 'Ballad' capture the Sweeney Todds of George Dibdin Pitt and Frederick Hazleton, the Sweeney Todds of Brian Burton and Austin Rosser, and the movie Sweeneys played by Tod Slaughter (1936) and Moore Marriott (1928). The Sweeney of the 'Ballad' is a mythical, larger-than-life character, and this is made explicit in the musical's epilogue, in which the chorus tells us that 'the more he bleeds, the more he lives' and warns us that 'Perhaps today you gave a nod / To Sweeney Todd' (190). The Sweeney of the 'Ballad' is immortal, undying. He 'wishes the world away' in the present tense, 'Hugging the blade' and 'waiting the years' (190). At the end of the musical we have just watched Tobias slit Sweeney's throat, but the chorus speaks of Sweeney as if he were still alive and, in fact, he is.

In the previous chapter I made the same distinction between the Sweeney of the 'Ballad' and the Sweeney in the musical, the man who sings 'My Friends' and 'Epiphany' and 'Johanna'. I noted there that the Sweeney we meet – unlike the Sweeney of the 'Ballad' – is a vulnerable and partially broken man whose body is incomplete and who attempts to reconstruct a self through acts of violence. I want, however, to attend further to this difference between the Sweeney we know and the Sweeney of the 'Ballad'.

Steve Swayne imagines that 'characters in a Sondheim musical who are wedded to place (such as an old theater or Japan or an island in the middle of Paris), [...] must explore and conquer the past in order to move hesitantly into the future'.[17] If the Sweeney of the 'Ballad' is somehow a ghost or one of the undead, might we perhaps think of Sweeney as needing to 'explore and conquer the past' in order to move on? Might the show framed and contained by the 'Ballad' be a kind of ritual performance and re-performance that is different every time and doesn't need to end the way it does?

The differences between the Sweeney we know and the Sweeney in the 'Ballad' suggest that this change has already begun to happen, that Sweeney has started to perform his story with a difference. At the beginning, the Sweeney of the 'Ballad' tells us 'What happened then – well that's the play / And he wouldn't want us to give it away', and, although this is a nod to the fact that everything has its price in the capitalist world of *Sweeney Todd*, it may also be true that *the story could turn out differently this time* (4). Indeed, *Sweeney Todd* as we know it already differs considerably from the story as it was originally told in *The String of Pearls*.

In Raymond Knapp's excellent discussion of *Sweeney*'s music, he argues that the 'Ballad' 'conjures Sweeney from his grave […] by re-creating the world in his image, with that image being above all a musical one, sustained through an incessant flow of leitmotiv-saturated music'. The musical, as Knapp sees it, is an extension of Sweeney's own dark sensibilities, and so

> it seems virtually inevitable that his death at the end does not truly finish him. As in countless horror films – which work essentially in the same way, and often just as carefully coordinated with music – the dominant malevolent presence cannot die at the end, so deeply intertwined is it within the world we have come to know. Even after his death, Sweeney's ongoing music asserts that the world has fully become his world, and once again conjures him from the grave, with the force of inexorable fate.[18]

But perhaps it is we who conjure Sweeney, not the other way around. Sweeney never demands that the chorus tell his story; it is they who demand something from him. Perhaps Prince's comment that the giant factory onstage makes Sweeney Todds is more than just an artful dodge. As I argued in the previous chapter, Sweeney is a *product* of his world; he has not made the world in his image. He *serves* a hungry god; he is not one himself.

The moment in the show in which Sweeney holds his right arm up as complete – with razor in hand – is underlined musically by the first return of the 'Ballad'. The company sings 'Lift your razor high, Sweeney! / Hear it singing, "Yes!" / Sink it in the rosy skin / Of righteousness!' (23). The chorus's other repetitions of the 'Ballad' (as at 54, 67, 144, 163) begin with narration; they tell us *about* Sweeney. Here, however, we find the chorus *aligned* with the character, encouraging him, even instructing him. The chorus speaks directly to Sweeney in the present tense and tells him what to do. They *want* Sweeney to lift his razor, to dispatch the Beadle, to float his blade across the throats of hypocrites. This is no chorus of dispassionate observers. It is a chorus of storytellers who agree with the malcontent of *The Revenger's Tragedy* when he says that 'When the bad bleeds, then is the tragedy good'.[19]

Examined in this way, we may find *Sweeney Todd* similar to one of Brecht's teaching plays, in which a character fails a battery of tests and consequently learns a series of lessons. Brecht's plays emphasize choices that could have been made differently, and it is possible to look at *Sweeney* in just this way. Maybe our undead character is doomed, like the captain of the *Flying Dutchman*, to re-enact the story until he solves a particular problem – until he doesn't kill Lucy, perhaps, or refuses to seek revenge in the first place.

It is tragic that he kills Lucy and that he murders Mrs Lovett, but, as Millie Taylor says, 'the highpoint of this tragedy is Todd's realization of his crimes in the final scene, the return of the music "There was a barber and his wife"', right before the epilogue brings back the narrative frame.[20] When the phrase 'There was a barber and his wife' returns, it seems, at first, as though it has returned with a difference. Musically, in fact, it would make sense for the lyrics to have changed. 'There was a barber and his wife', Sweeney sings, and then he tells us that 'She was beautiful / And she was virtuous / And he was – (*Shrugs*) / Naive' (186). This pause and shrug before the final 'naive' imply that Sweeney might be about to choose another word, one that explains his actions or one that shows more self-awareness. This pause opens up the possibility that Sweeney will tell us something that he learned over the course of the evening's re-enactment of the Sweeney Todd story, some new realization at which he has arrived.

But no. He returns to his song defeated. He says 'naive' again after all. And now Tobias will slit the barber's throat and the ritual will need to be performed again. It is this *return* that is the tragedy. Sweeney has killed before, we know from the 'Ballad', and he will probably kill again. The tragedy is that he didn't have to – doesn't have to.

Sweeney has seemed to many a show without optimism, a portrait of an industrialized world in which freedom is not possible and everything bends towards destruction. And it is true that this narrative is one with very little hope. But *Sweeney Todd* is a fable or tale – the 'Ballad' insists on this – and this is a story that has been told countless times and with many different variations. Thinking about the show as the repetition of a ritual opens up space for the hope that Anthony's name promises. *The tale can be told differently.* Ours is a demon barber who dreams of a world better than this one, 'If only angels could prevail' (131). The ritual might one day work. And if Sweeney hasn't accomplished the ritual the right way tonight, the possibility still exists of him doing it correctly tomorrow. Perhaps the next time the company calls the barber up from the grave, they will say 'Swing your razor wide, Sweeney! / Hold it to the skies!' and perhaps some day soon Sweeney will simply refuse.

Notes

1 Sondheim, *Finishing the Hat*, 334.

2 Knapp 340.

3 William Shakespeare, *Titus Andronicus*, edited by Jonathan Bate (London: Arden, 1995), 5.2.186–195.

4 William Shakespeare, *Timon of Athens*, edited by Anthony B. Dawson and Gretchen E. Minton (London: Arden, 2008), 1.2.39–45.

5 Michel de Montaigne, "Of Cannibals," in *The Complete Essays of Montaigne*, translated by Donald M. Frame (Stanford: Stanford University Press, 1958), 155.

6 Montaigne 156.

7 Montaigne 159.

8 Gordon 237.

9 David Savran and Daniel Gundlach, "*Anyone Can Whistle* as Experimental Theater," in *The Oxford Handbook of Sondheim Studies*, edited by Robert Gordon (Oxford: Oxford University Press, 2014), 81.

10 Kroll 101.

11 Rosalind Crone, *Violent Victorians: Popular Entertainment in Nineteenth-Century London* (Manchester: Manchester University Press, 2012), 184.

12 Bond, *Sweeney*, 3.

13 Sally Powell, "Black Markets and Cadaverous Pies: the Corpse, Urban Trade and Industrial Consumption in the Penny Blood," *Victorian Crime, Madness and Sensation*, edited by Andrew Maunder and Grace Moore (Aldershot: Ashgate, 2004), 49.

14 See Neil L. Whitehead, *Dark Shamans: Kanaimà and the Poetics of Violent Death* (Durham: Duke University Press, 2002).

15 See also Allen W. Menton, "Maternity, Madness, and Art in the Theater of Stephen Sondheim," in *Reading Stephen Sondheim*, edited by Sandor Goodhart (New York: Garland, 2000), 72.

16 Crone 200.

17 Swayne 188.
18 Knapp 337.
19 Middleton 3.5.202.
20 Millie Taylor, "*Sweeney Todd*: from Melodrama to Musical Tragedy," in *The Oxford Handbook of Sondheim Studies*, edited by Robert Gordon (Oxford: Oxford University Press, 2014), 347.

References

Arnold, Malcolm (1989). *Sweeney Todd: Ballet for Orchestra, Op. 68.* London: Faber Music.

Arrowsmith, William (1959). "Introduction to the *Bacchae*." In *Euripides V.* Edited by David Grene and Richmond Lattimore. Chicago: University of Chicago Press. 142–153.

Banfield, Stephen (1993). *Sondheim's Broadway Musicals.* Ann Arbor: University of Michigan Press.

Banfield, Stephen (2014). "Sondheim's Genius." In *The Oxford Handbook of Sondheim Studies.* Edited by Robert Gordon. Oxford: Oxford University Press. 11–24.

Barnes, Clive (1979). "Sondheim's *Sweeney Todd* Is a Bloody Good Musical." *New York Post.* 2 March. 29.

Berkvist, Robert (1979). "Stephen Sondheim Takes a Stab at Grand Guignol." *New York Times.* 25 February. D1, D5.

Bersani, Leo and Ulysse Dutoit (1985). *Forms of Violence: Narrative in Assyrian Art and Modern Culture.* New York: Schocken Books.

Blyton, Carey (1984). "Sondheim's *Sweeney Todd*: the Case for the Defence." *Tempo* 149: 19–26.

Bond, Christopher G. (1974). *Sweeney Todd: the Demon Barber of Fleet Street.* London: Samuel French.

Bond, Christopher G. (1991). "Introduction." In *Sweeney Todd: the Demon Barber of Fleet Street* by Stephen Sondheim and Hugh Wheeler. New York: Applause. 1–9.

Brecht, Bertolt (1964). "The Modern Theatre Is the Epic Theatre." Translated by John Willett. In *Brecht on Theatre: the Development of an Aesthetic.* Edited by John Willett. New York: Hill and Wang. 33–42.

Burton, Brian J. (1962). *Sweeney Todd the Barber: a Melodrama.* London: Samuel French.

Clurman, Harold (1979). Reviews of *Sweeney Todd* and *Strangers. Nation.* 24 March. 315–316.

Crone, Rosalind (2012). *Violent Victorians: Popular Entertainment in Nineteenth-Century London.* Manchester: Manchester University Press.

Cryer, Gretchen (1979). "On Collaboration between Authors and Directors." *Dramatists Guild Quarterly* 16, no. 2: 14–34.

Dibdin Pitt, George (1974). *The String of Pearls (Sweeney Todd).* In *The Golden Age of Melodrama: Twelve 19th Century Melodramas.* Edited by Michael Kilgarriff. London: Wolfe. 237–276.

Ellis-Fermor, Una (1965). *The Jacobean Drama.* 5th edn. London: Methuen.

Feingold, Michael (1979). "Sondheim, Bloody Sondheim." *Village Voice.* 12 March. 85.

Fenton, James (1980). "The Barberous Crimes of Sondheim and Prince." *Sunday Times* (London). 6 July. 40.

Foucault, Michel (1979). *Discipline and Punish: the Birth of the Prison.* Translated by Alan Sheridan. New York: Vintage.

Frazer, James George (1911). *Taboo and the Perils of the Soul.* 3rd edn. New York: St Martin's Press.

Fromm, Erich (1973). *The Anatomy of Human Destructiveness.* New York: Holt, Rinehart and Winston.

Gerould, Daniel C. (1980a). "Preface." *New York Literary Forum* 7: ix–xiii.

Gerould, Daniel C. (1980b). "A Toddography." *New York Literary Forum* 7: 43–48.

Goldberg, Jonathan (2016). *Melodrama: an Aesthetics of Impossibility.* Durham: Duke University Press.

Gordon, Joanne (1990). *Art Isn't Easy: the Achievement of Stephen Sondheim.* Carbondale: Southern Illinois University Press.

Gottfried, Martin (1999). *Balancing Act: the Authorized Biography of Angela Lansbury.* Boston: Little, Brown and Company.

Gottfried, Martin (2000). *Sondheim.* 2nd edn. New York: Harry N. Abrams.

Haag, Pamela (1999). *Consent: Sexual Rights and the Transformation of American Liberalism.* Ithaca: Cornell University Press.

Hand, Richard J. and Michael Wilson (2002). *Grand-Guignol: the French Theatre of Horror.* Exeter: University of Exeter Press.

Hardy, Thomas (1919). "The Blinded Bird." In *The Poetical Works of Thomas Hardy Vol. 1: Collected Poems, Lyrical, Narratory, and Reflective.* London: MacMillan and Co. 418–419.

Hazleton, Frederick (1862). *Sweeney Todd, the Barber of Fleet Street: or, The String of Pearls.* London: Samuel French.

Hirsch, Foster (2005). *Harold Prince and the American Musical Theatre.* 2nd edn. New York: Applause.

Horowitz, Mark Eden (2010). *Sondheim on Music: Minor Details and Major Decisions.* 2nd edn. Lanham: Scarecrow Press.

Hume, Tim (2016). "Teen Actors' Necks Slit in School Production of *Sweeney Todd.*" 8 April 2016. www.cnn.com/2016/04/07/asia/new-zealand-sweeney-todd-razor/index.html (accessed 1st February 2018).

Ilson, Carol (2000). *Harold Prince: a Director's Journey.* 2nd edn. New York: Limelight.

Kauffmann, Stanley (1979). "Slay It with Music." *New Republic.* 24 March. 24–25.

Kerr, Walter (1979). "Is Sweeney on Target?" *New York Times.* 11 March. D1, D4.

Knapp, Raymond (2006). *The American Musical and the Performance of Personal Identity.* Princeton: Princeton University Press.

Kristeva, Julia (1982). *Powers of Horror: an Essay on Abjection.* Translated by Leon S. Roudiez. New York: Columbia University Press.

Kroll, Jack (1979). "The Blood Runs Cold." *Newsweek.* 12 March. 101–103.

Lahr, John (1979). "Sondheim's Little Deaths: the Ironic Mode and Its Discontents." *Harper's* 258, no. 4: 71–78.

Lahr, John (2015). *Joy Ride: Show People and Their Shows.* New York: Norton.

Logan, John (2006). *Sweeney Todd: the Demon Barber of Fleet Street.* www.joblo.com/scripts/script_sweeneytodd.pdf (accessed 15 July 2017).

Mack, Robert L., ed. (2007a). *Sweeney Todd: the Demon Barber of Fleet Street.* Oxford: Oxford University Press.

Mack, Robert L. (2007b). *The Wonderful and Surprising History of Sweeney Todd: the Life and Times of an Urban Legend.* London: Continuum.

Marchesani, Joseph (2000). "Arresting Development: Law, Love, and the Name-of-the-Father in *Sweeney Todd*." In *Reading Stephen Sondheim*. Edited by Sandor Goodhart. New York: Garland. 171–185.

Menton, Allen W. (2000). "Maternity, Madness, and Art in the Theater of Stephen Sondheim." In *Reading Stephen Sondheim*. Edited by Sandor Goodhart. New York: Garland. 61–76.

Middleton, Thomas (2007). *The Revenger's Tragedy*. Edited by MacDonald P. Jackson. In *Thomas Middleton: the Collected Works*. Edited by Gary Taylor and John Lavagnino. Oxford: Clarendon. 543–593.

Miller, Peter and Randall Lewton (1980). *The Sweeney Todd Shock 'n' Roll Show*. London: Samuel French.

Mollin, Alfred (1991). "Mayhem and Morality in *Sweeney Todd*." *American Music* 9, no. 4: 405–417.

Montaigne, Michel de (1958). "Of Cannibals." In *The Complete Essays of Montaigne*. Translated by Donald M. Frame. Stanford: Stanford University Press. 150–159.

Munk, Erika (1979). "Sondheim, Bloody Sondheim." *Village Voice*. 12 March. 85–86.

Novick, Julius (1979). "Sondheim, Bloody Sondheim." *Village Voice*. 12 March. 85.

Ovid (2010). *Metamorphoses*. Translated by Stanley Lombardo. Indianapolis: Hackett Publishing.

Powell, Sally (2004). "Black Markets and Cadaverous Pies: the Corpse, Urban Trade and Industrial Consumption in the Penny Blood." *Victorian Crime, Madness and Sensation*. Edited by Andrew Maunder and Grace Moore. Aldershot: Ashgate. 45–58.

Reed, Rex (1979). "Sweeney Soars." *Daily News*. 4 March. 7, 13.

Rosser, Austin (1971). *Sweeney Todd: a Victorian Melodrama*. London: Samuel French.

Savran, David and Daniel Gundlach (2014). "*Anyone Can Whistle* as Experimental Theater." In *The Oxford Handbook of Sondheim Studies*. Edited by Robert Gordon. Oxford: Oxford University Press. 81–94.

Shakespeare, William (1995). *Titus Andronicus*. Edited by Jonathan Bate. London: Arden.

Shakespeare, William (2008). *Timon of Athens*. Edited by Anthony B. Dawson and Gretchen E. Minton. London: Arden.

Simkins, Michael (2008). "Slitting Your Throat and Other Theatrical Hazards." 11 December 2008. www.theguardian.com/stage/theatreblog/2008/dec/11/theatre-slit-throat-austrian-actor (1 February 2018).

Simon, John (1979). "A Little Knife Music." *New York* [magazine]. 19 March. 74–75.

Sondheim, Stephen (1980). "Larger than Life: Reflections on Melodrama and Sweeney Todd." *New York Literary Forum* 7: 3–14.

Sondheim, Stephen (1999). *Sweeney Todd: the Demon Barber of Fleet Street* [Score]. New York: Rilting Music.

Sondheim, Stephen (2010). *Finishing the Hat: Collected Lyrics (1954–1981) with Attendant Comments, Principles, Heresies, Grudges, Whines and Anecdotes*. New York: Knopf.

Sondheim, Stephen (2011). *Look, I Made a Hat: Collected Lyrics (1981–2011) with Attendant Comments, Amplifications, Dogmas, Harangues, Digressions, Anecdotes and Miscellany*. New York: Knopf.

Sondheim, Stephen and Hugh Wheeler (1979). *Sweeney Todd: the Demon Barber of Fleet Street*. New York: Mead, Dodd & Company.

Sutton, Martyn (1980). "How to Write a Musical without Big Numbers." *Sunday Times* (London). 6 July. 40.

Swayne, Steve (2005). *How Sondheim Found His Sound*. Ann Arbor: University of Michigan Press.

Taylor, Millie (2014). "*Sweeney Todd*: from Melodrama to Musical Tragedy." In *The Oxford Handbook of Sondheim Studies*. Edited by Robert Gordon. Oxford: Oxford University Press. 335–349.

Wallop, Harry (2014). "Why French Chefs Want Us to Eat This Bird – Head, Bones, Beak and All." 18 September 2014. www.telegraph.co.uk/foodanddrink/11102100/Why-French-chefs-want-us-to-eat-this-bird-head-bones-beak-and-all.html (1 February 2018)

Webster, John (2009). *The Duchess of Malfi*. Edited by Leah S. Marcus. London: Arden.

Whitehead, Neil L. (2002). *Dark Shamans: Kanaimà and the Poetics of Violent Death*. Durham: Duke University Press.

Williams, Bernard (1993). *Shame and Necessity*. Berkeley: University of California Press.

Zadan, Craig (1989). *Sondheim & Co.* 2nd edn. New York: Harper & Row.

Zakariasen, Bill (1979). "*Sweeney* Returns Opera to Its Roots." *Daily News* (New York). 4 June. 25.

Index